Drawn
to the
Civil War

ALSO BY J. STEPHEN LANG

The Complete Book of Confederate Trivia

The Big Book of American Trivia

The Complete Book of Bible Trivia

*The One Hundred Most Important
Events in Christian History* (co-author)

Biblical Quotations for All Occasions

John F. Blair
Publisher
Winston-Salem, North Carolina

Drawn to the Civil War

Text by J. Stephen Lang

Illustrations by
Michael Caplanis

DESIGN BY DEBRA LONG HAMPTON

PRINTED AND BOUND BY R. R. DONNELLEY & SONS

*The paper in this book meets the guidelines
for permanence and durability
of the Committee on Production Guidelines
for Book Longevity of the Council on Library Resources.*

Library of Congress Cataloging-in-Publication Data

Lang, J. Stephen.
Drawn to the Civil War / text by Stephen Lang ; illustrations by Michael Caplanis.
p.   cm.
Includes bibliographical references (p.   ) and index.
ISBN 0-89587-186-6 (alk. paper)
1. United States—History—Civil War, 1861–1865—Biography—Anecdotes.
2. United States—History—Civil War, 1861–1865—Biography—Caricatures and cartoons.
3. American wit and humor, Pictorial.
I. Caplanis, Michael, 1951–
II. Title.
E467.L35 1999
973.7′092′2—dc21
[B]   99-047248

For Wightman Weese,
witty and wise

J. S. L.

For Karen and Jean

M. C.

Contents

Introduction

OVER THE YEARS, millions of American school-children have slept their way through United States history classes. They have driven their poor teachers to distraction and emerged with a knowledge of history that would fit on a Post-It note. How is it that they have turned into adults who buy Civil War books and videotapes by the truckload? Did they begin to wonder if America's past was really worth knowing? Did a search for their roots make them dig into the years from 1861 to 1865? Did all those PBS specials—plus the Learning Channel, the History Channel, and all the others—turn yawners into people who love the past?

Who can tell? The fact is, Americans (and quite a few people abroad) can't get enough of the Civil War. For many scholars and experts, it is their lifework. But a lot of people are dabblers who enjoy playing with the past. History experts look at them the way preachers look at people who read the Bible once a month. They aren't true believers if they're only dipping their toes in the pool.

But dabbling is fun. Most people don't want a thick book about the Civil War.

They're satisfied with the basics. Who were the key figures? What were the key issues? Which were the major battles? Cut to the chase. Give us the Civil War in a nutshell. After all, we're not scholars.

But brief biographies of major Civil War figures can be as dull as dishwater—unless you give the reader "the rest of the story," to borrow Paul Harvey's famous phrase. In fact, Civil War generals, politicians, and other key players were definitely *not* boring. They were as quirky and fascinating as any major media figures today. So a good book about them should tell you not simply the facts that make their way into encyclopedias but also the kind of curious, odd, up-close-and-personal tidbits that make human beings, well, human. It's fine to know that Stonewall Jackson was a superb military leader and one of the best infantry strategists of all time. But learning about Jackson the tone-deaf hymn singer, the diet and exercise fanatic, the hypochondriac, the humorless church deacon, the doting husband, the wounded warrior who prayed he would die on a Sunday—now, *that's* a more interesting picture. *That's* a character we're drawn to.

So, for the pleasure of both dabblers and devotees, we present *Drawn to the Civil War*— "the rest of the story" about Robert E. Lee, Abe Lincoln, William T. Sherman, Jefferson Davis,

and some lesser-known but intriguing characters like spy Rose Greenhow and guerrilla leader Bill Quantrill. We apologize for having to omit some noteworthy figures, but we're confident in saying that all those we've included are, in the opinion of historians, important to know about. Scholars are welcome to check the facts, for we have done our homework. But our focus is clearly on the human beings—warts, quirks, and all.

And in case you haven't noticed, we've also given you pictures—not the official portraits you'll find in reference books, but something better and more revealing: caricatures. They should serve as a reminder that a cartoon can often capture an individual better than a camera can. And here's a bit of historical trivia: during the Civil War, newspapers and magazines weren't yet able to print photographs. For the people of the day, images of important people were given in the form of caricatures. Naturally, the Yanks liked to show the Rebels as grotesque and silly, and the Rebels returned the favor. That is one way we prove our humanity: by keeping a sense of humor about something very serious.

"Of making many books there is no end; and much study is a weariness of the flesh." So said the wise Solomon, according to the Bible. Could he have predicted how many thousands of books would be published about a wasteful four-year war that divided a nation and still causes heated discussion? Maybe not. But study does not have to bring weariness of the flesh. It can be fun. That is our aim here—to amuse as well as to inform.

So we invite you to meet the people of the Civil War—both in words and pictures. For those of you who yawned or slept your way through history class, here is history for the sheer enjoyment of it.

Drawn
to the
Civil War

Robert Anderson, Union Officer
(1805–1871)

IN THE THICK OF THE BEGINNING

EVERYONE KNOWS that the whole thing began with the firing on Fort Sumter. What everyone forgets is that the decrepit old pile of rock wasn't very important in itself. It just happened to be a piece of Federal turf that lay offshore from Secession City—Charleston, South Carolina. The secessionist hotheads couldn't tolerate a Union military post staring at them from Charleston Harbor. Poor Major Robert Anderson, the Union commander of the fort, had the fortune—or misfortune—to be the man of the hour, the first Yankee hero of the war. Why the North treated him as a hero when he surrendered the fort is one of those peculiar puzzles of fame, timing, and the public's need to idolize.

Anderson was Kentucky-born, from

Virginia stock. He married a Georgia woman. He was also a former slave owner and a man who had no real beef against slavery . . . or secession. It was one of the war's many delightful ironies that a Southern boy happened to be commanding the Union fort that the newly formed Confederacy insisted on having.

He was probably wise enough to know the fort had minimal military value. Yet there it was, staring across the water at a seceded state and flying the United States flag. Sumter had become a symbol. That detested flag had to go.

Anderson's presence in Charleston was no accident. He had been sent there in November 1860 by James Buchanan's secretary of war, John Floyd, a Virginian and later a Confederate general. Floyd was a devious and decidedly pro-Southern man who saw war looming and guessed how important Sumter would be. It was widely believed that he sent the Southern-born Anderson there in the hope that he would betray the fort and "turn Rebel" at the right moment. It didn't quite work that way.

Often forgotten in this familiar tale is Anderson's first assignment in the Charleston area—he and his men were stationed at Fort Moultrie on the mainland. In December 1860, South Carolina seceded and declared itself an independent republic, at least until there were enough seceded states to form a confederacy. When the South Carolinians made Anderson and his Federals feel uneasy at Fort Moultrie, they moved to Fort Sumter on its man-made island—safer, perhaps, but still sitting on a powder keg.

Before Lincoln took office, President James Buchanan sent the *Star of the West* to bring supplies to Fort Sumter. The South Carolinians saw this as a hostile act (like practically everything else the Union did), and Charleston's shore artillery fired on the ship, forcing it to turn back. The *Star* only appeared to be a merchant ship; the Federals had outfitted it with troops and armaments, so it was in effect a warship. Buchanan's administration sent Anderson instructions to return fire if the *Star* was fired on—but these instructions arrived after the ship was gone. Some count the firing on the *Star* as the actual first shots of the war.

In Montgomery, Alabama, in April 1861, Jefferson Davis and his cabinet debated the Sumter issue nervously. The boozy but sometimes sensible secretary of state, Robert Toombs, paced the room and predicted—correctly—that "the firing upon that fort will inaugurate a civil war. . . . It is suicide, murder, and will lose us every friend in the North. . . . It is unnecessary,

ROBERT
ANDERSON

1805–1871

it puts us in the wrong, it is fatal." All true, but the cabinet voted to take the fort anyway. A message was sent to the feisty Beauregard in Charleston: Demand surrender of the fort, and if refused, "reduce it."

General Beauregard sent his aides to Anderson on April 11, 1861, demanding surrender. Anderson refused. (This was the part of the story that made him a hero in the North's eyes.) He also made a practical observation: his food was running out. (Needless to say, no Charleston market was supplying provisions.) His men, Anderson said, would be "starved out in a few days." This news went via Beauregard to the cabinet, which then ordered Beauregard to avoid bloodshed if possible. But negotiations between Anderson and the Rebels broke down, partly because Anderson said he would willingly evacuate in three days—unless he received additional supplies, that is. The cabinet plainly told Beauregard he must not allow Anderson to receive provisions.

So it was that Anderson was informed at three-thirty on the morning of April 12, 1861, that firing would commence in one hour. The deeply religious man said to the Confederate agents, "If we never meet in this world again, God grant that we may meet in the next."

The firing did commence—and continued for the next thirty-four hours. (Tradition has it that the Union's first shot was fired by Anderson's second-in-command, Abner Doubleday, who is credited—incorrectly—with inventing baseball.) Cannonballs battered the fort's brick walls, and "hot shot" set fire to the wooden buildings inside. Anderson's men suffered smoke inhalation. No Union aid showed up.

Around one o'clock on the afternoon of April 13, Anderson surrendered, minutes after the Union flag was shot down. Not a very theatrical personality, he told Beauregard's representatives, "Gentlemen, this is a very awkward business." The man who negotiated with Anderson was James Chesnut, husband of the more famous Mary Chesnut, keeper of the war's most-read diary. In his trunk, Anderson had the Union flag he had defended, burnt and shot through. He vowed to have it wrapped around him when laid in his grave.

After leaving South Carolina (no doubt with much relief), Anderson was the toast of the North. Arriving in New York on April 23, he was greeted as a hero at a pro-Union gathering of fifty thousand. The modest man must have been smiling inside; he was only a symbol, just like Fort Sumter. He had been there when the South fired the first shot, and he had resisted as long as he could. While the

South cheered Beauregard, the North cheered the man who surrendered. Lincoln made him a brigadier general.

Still, Anderson faced a dilemma. He was still, and always would be, a Southerner, and he feared that his home state of Kentucky might join the Confederacy. He made a vow: if Kentucky seceded, he would go to Europe "to become a spectator of the contest, and not an actor."

Kentucky did not secede, though it was a deeply divided state that sent representatives to the Congresses of both the U.S.A. and the C.S.A. Anderson was given command of Federal troops in his native state and was thus briefly forced to be an actor, and not a spectator. But he was fortunate. Ill health put him out of commission for most of the war.

Fast-forward to April 14, 1865, when Anderson returned to Fort Sumter, which had been recaptured by the Union. He hoisted the Union flag over it once more. Later that day, Lincoln was shot. It was exactly four years since Anderson had departed the fort.

Anderson died, appropriately enough, in Charleston.

$\mathcal{P}$. G. T. Beauregard, Confederate General

(1818–1893)

LITTLE BEAU PEEVED

EGOS, NOT GUNS, might be the loudest things in war. If Pierre Gustave Toutant Beauregard didn't have the loudest ego, he at least possessed the longest name. Of course, he had a lot to be vain about—directing the bombing of Fort Sumter, putting on a grand show at First Manassas, designing the Confederate Battle Flag. Had his accomplishments matched his ego (hardly possible), he would have achieved even more.

The general with the long name was a short man, five-foot-seven, with the ego that often accompanies lack of physical stature. He was of old Creole stock, born on a plantation south of New Orleans. He spoke French before he learned English.

That proved useful when he was at West Point, since the classics in the art of war were in French. (French was in those days the language of war, not love or cuisine.) He was a disciple of Napoleon and military theorist Henri de Jomini. But wanting to seem more "Anglo," he changed his last name (it was actually Toutant-Beauregard) and dropped the Pierre, signing himself G. T. Beauregard.

G. T. B. was second in the class of 1838. During the Mexican War (a prep course for future Civil War officers), he served as an engineer under Winfield Scott, whom he impressed. Scott called him a "bulldog with his ears pinned back." But Beauregard held a grudge against Scott, who had not commended him as highly as he did others (notably Robert E. Lee and George McClellan). It was not the last time Beauregard's pride was wounded.

After Mexico, he impressed New Orleans residents with his military engineering—but failed in his bid to be mayor there in 1858. He pulled some family strings (his wife's sister's husband was Senator John Slidell) and was appointed to head West Point—but served only a few days before it was learned he was pro-secession. When Louisiana did secede, he scurried home, expecting a commission as commander of the state's military—but

Braxton Bragg got the post. Not wanting any commission if he couldn't have the top slot, the peevish Beauregard enlisted as a private. Slidell recommended Private Beauregard to President Davis, who made him a brigadier general and placed him in a fateful post: Charleston.

In April 1861, the fame seeker found what he wanted. In directing the Confederate bombardment of Fort Sumter, he touched off the Civil War and made himself the first hero of the Confederacy. Southern newspapers couldn't say enough good things about "Old Bory." The editor of one Northern newspaper advertised a bounty on his head.

Old Bory rode in triumph to Richmond, where, in false humility, he refused to ride in a spangled carriage. The public praised this mock modesty.

More glory followed. Jefferson Davis feared for Richmond's safety (as did Richmond) and assigned Beauregard to stop the Yankees at the north. Showing his flair for public relations, he summoned the citizens near Manassas, Virginia, to be present as the Rebels fought off their Yankee foes. The people loved it.

At Manassas, Beauregard was technically second in command to General Joseph Johnston. But Johnston understood that

P. G. T.
BEAUREGARD

1818–1893

Beauregard knew the terrain better, so in effect, Old Bory oversaw the Confederate forces. Beauregard actually asked Johnston to leave the field when the fighting began.

The battle was a smashing victory and a great Southern morale booster. Jefferson Davis made Beauregard a full general the next day. Before the battle, Beauregard had told his men, "Let tomorrow be their Waterloo." It wasn't quite that final, but it did earn the South's applause.

The French tend to be tidy minded and detail oriented. Beauregard certainly was. Aware at Manassas that friend and foe were easily confused due to the similarity of the two armies' flags, he supposedly designed the famous Rebel Battle Flag, a legacy that has endured.

Feeling cocky because of all this acclaim, Beauregard fell to loggerheads with the Confederate War Department. Davis sent him west to serve under Albert Sidney Johnston. Rumor was that Beauregard wanted the office of Confederate president.

Beauregard assumed command when Johnston was killed at the Battle of Shiloh in Tennessee. He wired Richmond that Shiloh was a victory—something of an exaggeration. Davis blamed Beauregard for not following up by pursuing the Federals. Old Bory's order for

his frazzled troops to rest instead of chasing the Yankees was perhaps the most fateful of his life, for it permanently soured Davis.

Later, Beauregard found a niche that he loved: directing the defenses at Charleston. His love affair with the locals endured from his Fort Sumter success. He was haughty and vain—something Charlestonians completely understood and appreciated.

"The Grand Creole," as some called him (and as he no doubt saw himself), had a Frenchman's love of words—the more, the better. His communications to officers were very long and very detailed. His dispatches to the government in Richmond could be laughably self-promoting—for example, one was marked "Centreville, Va., within the sound of the enemy's guns." Old Bory had a neurotic fear that someone might disregard his greatness. And he had a flair for the dramatic. In Tennessee, he issued an appeal for civilians to donate their plantation bells to be made into cannon.

Because of his vanity and temper, he locked horns with Confederate bigwigs. Toward the end of the war, he was given an administrative post in the western Confederacy, a position of little power.

Postwar, he fared better, serving as president of a railway, then making mega-money as a supervisor—along with fellow Confederate veteran Jubal Early—of the Louisiana State Lottery. Still, Beauregard felt a need to defend his war record. In a reversal of ghost writing, he published, under a friend's name, *The Military Operations of General Beauregard*, in which he defended his actions and lamented how underappreciated the magnificent General Beauregard was.

A historical note: Old Bory was no prophet. In 1868, he claimed that there were a half-million fewer blacks in the Gulf States than there had been in 1860. "They are dying fast," he wrote. "In seventy-five years hence they will have vanished from this continent along with the red man and the buffalo."

Judah P. Benjamin, Confederate Politician
(1811–1884)

THE PERPETUAL SMILE

WHAT DID HIS perpetual half-smile indicate? Superiority? Amusement? Bliss? No one knew, or ever will, for in post-Confederate days, Judah P. Benjamin made a new life in another country.

He was a Jew, born a British subject in the Virgin Islands. But he became a true Southerner with roots in Charleston and New Orleans and a deep love for Southern plantation life. His marriage to a Creole aristocrat led to financial rewards and a life in politics. In 1852, he became the first Jew elected to the United States Senate, where he was noted as a fine orator and defender of Southern interests. After Senator Jefferson Davis of Mississippi supposedly insulted him on the Senate floor, Benjamin challenged him to a duel. Davis apologized publicly for the insult, and he and Benjamin then became close friends.

Benjamin's wife, Natalie, preferred Paris to Louisiana or Washington. Benjamin saw her only during his annual trips to Paris. There were scandalous rumors about her in Washington, but no one ever learned the real nature of their long-distance marriage.

He had the admiration of his colleagues, but sometimes his Jewishness became an issue. Senator Ben Wade of Ohio accused Benjamin of being an "Israelite with Egyptian principles." Benjamin usually responded to insults with his smile, but in this case, he told the Senate that while his ancestors were receiving the Ten Commandments from God, "the ancestors of my opponent were herding swine in the forests of Great Britain."

During the secession crisis, Benjamin went with the South. Former Senate colleague Davis, now president of the Confederacy, made him the new nation's first attorney general. Benjamin's hard work and delight in details led to his being called the "Poo Bah" of the Confederacy. While heading the South's Justice Department, Benjamin advocated "cotton diplomacy"—shipping cotton to Europe in exchange for arms and supplies and with-

holding it from nations that did not support the South.

Then he got a new slot: secretary of war. Considering he had no military experience, this shocked many. But it made sense, because Davis—a Mexican War veteran and the United States secretary of war under Franklin Pierce—was really his own secretary of war. Officially, Benjamin was the military man in the cabinet, meaning that as things went wrong on the battlefield, he was the one to blame. Some generals who dared not attack the Confederacy's president found it convenient to scapegoat Benjamin. To Confederate military men, he was a civilian amateur, and no amount of hard work on his part could make up for his being a nonsoldier.

Benjamin put in fourteen-hour days and quarreled with such generals as Stonewall Jackson and P. G. T. Beauregard. Jackson threatened to resign because he couldn't tolerate Benjamin's "interference in my command." Beauregard called the secretary "that functionary at his desk." Joe Johnston wrote his wife, "If that miserable little Jew is retained in his place, our country will never be able to defend itself." Yet Davis dutifully defended the dutiful Benjamin—rightly so, since Benjamin was only following the president's orders.

Following the South's loss of Roanoke Is-

JUDAH P.
BENJAMIN

1811–1884

land, North Carolina, Benjamin resigned as secretary of war. Davis wisely replaced him with a military man, then moved Benjamin to secretary of state. There, he faced the South's key public relations problem: Europe frowned on a nation that tolerated slavery (Benjamin himself had 140 slaves on his sugar plantation). He had a brainstorm. To get Europeans (especially the English) on the Confederate side, the South should offer to free any slaves who would fight with the Rebels. Benjamin had Robert E. Lee's backing, but almost no one else's. When he delivered a speech on this radical notion in Richmond, ten thousand people heard him—and practically no one agreed. Even so, the Confederate Congress approved the notion in March 1865—too late to matter, since the surrender at Appomattox followed a month later.

After the war, the government in Washington was fairly kind to former Confederate officers—but not to Confederate politicians. Like the other cabinet members, Benjamin was under suspicion of having some connection to John Wilkes Booth. He fled to England, taking the time to burn most of his personal papers (he burned the rest just before his death). If he did this to keep historians guessing about him, he succeeded.

Benjamin began practicing law in England

after living there only five months. He was a smashing success in his new life—and he completely put aside the old one, never writing or speaking about the Confederacy. With one exception, that is. Just after arriving in England, he wrote a letter protesting the imprisonment of his old friend Jefferson Davis. When Davis later visited London, he and Benjamin dined together. Davis was Benjamin's only contact from Confederate days.

He never returned to America. After retiring from the English bar, he moved to Paris to be with his family. He was buried in the famous Pere Lachaise cemetery under the name Philippe Benjamin (his middle name was Philip). Not satisfied with Benjamin's chosen anonymity, the Daughters of the Confederacy erected a monument there in the 1930s; it mentions his service to the Confederacy, among other achievements.

Years after the Confederacy ended, the former Confederate president called Benjamin "the most accomplished statesman I have ever known." Yet oddly, in his two-volume memoirs, Davis mentioned his old friend only in passing. Davis's wife, Varina, assured everyone that while the Confederacy existed, her husband and Judah Benjamin saw each other almost every day.

Benjamin was a nonpracticing Jew, yet he

never denied his Jewishness. Historians believe he was the most politically powerful Jew in American history.

Curiously, in his younger days, he had turned down an offer that would have changed the whole course of his life: President Millard Fillmore had wished to make him a Supreme Court justice.

John Wilkes Booth, Actor and Assassin
(1838–1865)

PLAYING FOR KEEPS

ABRAHAM LINCOLN was an avid theatergoer. The first time he saw *Hamlet*, which he loved, Edwin Booth played the lead.

Edwin was a member of one of the world's most renowned acting families. The head of the clan was Junius Brutus Booth, father of ten children, including Junius Jr., Edwin, and John. The elder Junius, born in London, was renowned in England for his masterful acting in Shakespeare's tragedies, but after 1821, he made America his home.

John, born in Maryland, studied theater in Baltimore and made his debut there. Like the other Booths, he earned his reputation in Shakespearean roles. He was handsome (women loved his hypnotic eyes) and had a beautiful speaking voice and an ability to change moods quickly and convincingly (probably rooted in his own temperament, which was noted for mood swings from depression to elation). John was also athletic; one theater critic called him "the gymnastic actor." He could leap over a five-foot piece of stage scenery with little effort.

Southern aristocrats loved him, and he felt a bond with that upper-class audience. Not surprisingly, he reacted with snobbery to the log-cabin-born Lincoln and made no attempt to hide his feelings: "This man's appearance, his pedigree, his coarse low jokes and anecdotes, his vulgar similes and his frivolity, are a disgrace to the seat he holds."

John told his adored sister Asia that he wished to go down in history as a *Southern* actor. After Fort Sumter fell, he was jubilant, telling Asia, "If the North conquer us, it will be by numbers only."

Asia noted that there was no "us"—the Booths were not Southerners, even though John had been born in Baltimore.

John replied, "So help me God, my soul, life, and possessions are for the South!"

He began to think of Lincoln not only as low-class but also as a tyrant and a vile enemy of liberty. He told his brother Edwin, "You will see Lincoln made a king in America." He also stated that slavery was the natural order of things and was the greatest gift "God ever

bestowed upon a favored nation." Lincoln's reelection in 1864 drove him almost mad, and he began to hatch a scheme to kidnap him from the White House and drag him off to Richmond, where he would serve as the ransom for all Confederate prisoners.

From the underbelly of Washington and Baltimore, he recruited a gang of losers and misfits, all haters of Lincoln, some of them probably one step away from the prison or asylum door. (This gang of cutthroats was not much different from John Brown's fanatical followers. Booth, who loathed all abolitionists, had been present at Brown's execution in 1859.) The conspirators studied floor plans of the White House and stalked the president. They were prepared to kidnap him a few days after his inauguration in March 1865, but the plan fell through. Some of the conspirators dropped out following that.

After Booth heard Lincoln's post-Appomattox speech, he hit on a new possibility: instead of kidnapping the president (which was obviously fraught with complications), he would simply kill him. By Good Friday, the plan was hatched. Booth would kill Lincoln, German immigrant George Atzerodt would kill Vice President Johnson, and hulking Lewis Powell would kill Secretary of State Seward. This would remove the top three executives

JOHN
WILKES
BOOTH

1838–1865

in the administration. (Had they used their brains, they would have seen that the South-hating secretary of war, Edwin Stanton, was a better choice than Johnson or Seward.)

What motivated Booth? Though he claimed to be a Southerner, he spent most of the war playing in Northern theaters. He began to feel guilt that he was doing nothing to aid the South, so the abduction—or killing—of the tyrant, Lincoln, would serve two purposes: it would be a great dramatic performance, and it would serve a blow to the Union.

The story of the assassination has been told and retold. Suffice it to say that Booth was a familiar face at Ford's Theatre, knew its floor plan, and had no trouble slipping inside that fateful night, Good Friday, April 14, 1865. The doorkeeper knew him, and he passed through easily: "You don't need a ticket, Buck." The play that night, a comedy, *Our American Cousin*, was one Booth knew by heart. He chose his moment with precision, when actor Harry Hawk was to be left alone on the stage. Hawk spoke the lines, "Don't know the manners of good society, eh? Wal, I guess I know enough to turn you inside out, old gal, you sockdologizing old mantrap. . . ." At that point, Booth opened the door to the theater box and shot Lincoln with a derringer in the back of the head. When he leaped from the box (remember, he was "the gymnastic actor"), his spur caught in a flag, and when he crash-landed on the stage, his left shinbone broke just above the ankle. The audience was puzzled. Here was the actor Booth—was this part of the play? Booth called out the state motto of Virginia: *"Sic semper tyrannis!"* ("Thus always to tyrants!"). He then hobbled off, left Ford's by its back door, and galloped away.

The Federal government, paranoid after the shooting, jailed the entire cast of *Our American Cousin*, suspecting the players might have known of the plot. Booth's gentle sister Asia was also jailed for a while. Brother Edwin announced he would take a long sabbatical from the American stage.

John Wilkes Booth was fascinated by himself (not a rarity among actors). Not surprisingly, he kept a diary. Thanks to it, we have some idea of what ran through his mind in those frantic days between Lincoln's death and his own. He expressed surprise that he wasn't hailed as a hero (even most die-hard Confederates were horrified at the shooting) but was rather being hunted down like a dog. "I can never repent it, though we hated to kill. Our country owed all our troubles to him, and God simply made me the instrument of his punishment. . . . I care not what becomes of me. I have no desire to outlive my country. . . . For my country I have given up all that makes life sweet and holy. . . . God, try and forgive me, and bless my mother."

A certain Southern-sympathizing doctor (his name was Mudd) set Booth's broken leg and made him a pair of crude crutches. Booth holed up in a tobacco barn in Virginia, where the Federals found him. His accomplice Davy Herold came out with his hands up, but Booth, carrying two guns, yelled, "Well, my brave boys, you can prepare a stretcher for me!" The Federals set the barn on fire to smoke him out, and one of them shot Booth. After being dragged from the burning barn, he gasped, "Tell my mother . . . Tell my mother that I died for my country." His last words (very appropriate ones) were "I thought I did for the best. . . . Useless . . . useless."

His body, sewn up in a bag, was brought to Secretary of War Stanton, who feared that Rebels might try to carry it off. He had Booth buried in secret under the floor at the Washington Arsenal. In 1869, the War Department allowed the body to be exhumed and reburied by Booth's family, who took it to Green Mount Cemetery in Baltimore.

Braxton Bragg, Confederate General
(1817–1876)

VICTIM (AND SOURCE) OF HEADACHES

LOOKING AT PHOTOGRAPHS of the mature Braxton Bragg, many people have thought he resembled a sullen gorilla—or a neanderthal. He definitely was not a happy man. Bragg was one of those pitiful souls who have talent and ambition but no people skills whatsoever. One teacher called the boy Braxton "a youth of tractable and docile disposition." It was probably the last time anyone spoke of him as "tractable and docile." Most were inclined to agree with U. S. Grant, who claimed that Bragg had "an irascible temper, and was naturally disputatious." He definitely had a chip on his shoulder. When a Charleston man called Bragg's home state of North Carolina "a strip of land between two states," Bragg challenged him to a duel. Yet when the Civil War began, the cantankerous Bragg was high on the Confederacy's most-likely-to-succeed list. Why?

Part of Bragg's legend involved his Mexican War service. Supposedly, the young Bragg helped win a key battle when he obeyed General Zachary Taylor's order: "A little more grape, Captain Bragg." ("Grape" was grapeshot, the iron balls that were standard ammunition.) Bragg himself related years later that Taylor actually said, "Give 'em hell, Bragg." But the much-repeated "grape story" had a special place in the heart of Jefferson Davis, whose first wife was Zachary Taylor's daughter. Davis considered Bragg a loyal friend. (During the Civil War, many considered Bragg to be Davis's pet, feeling that the bond between the two blurred Davis's objectivity toward Bragg's ability.)

In Mexico, someone tried to assassinate Bragg by putting a bomb under his bed, which somehow didn't injure him. One newspaper reported the incident and offered no motive except that "some of his men think he is too severe in his discipline." Bragg was a national hero following the "grape" incident, yet already his lack of tact was doing him harm.

While still basking in his fame, Bragg met his future wife at a Louisiana ball given in his honor. He married Elise, a plantation belle, bought a sixteen-hundred-acre sugar plantation, and gave it the unromantic (but very military) name Bivouac.

When the Civil War began, Bragg moved swiftly up the ladder. Davis appointed him a brigadier general. By early 1862, he was a full general. Davis told a private gathering at the Confederate White House that Bragg was "the only general in command of an army who had shown himself equal to the management of volunteers." Davis put him in charge of the western Confederacy.

Bragg thought an invasion of Kentucky would be wise. The campaign achieved nothing, in part because of difficulties between Bragg and General Leonidas Polk, an Episcopal bishop. (One interesting item in Kentucky: Bragg was in Frankfort presiding over the installation of Richard Hawes as Confederate governor of Kentucky when the ceremony was interrupted by the Federals.)

As commander of the Army of Tennessee, Bragg fared badly in the Volunteer State and elsewhere. The bloody battle at Murfreesboro began on December 31, 1862; Bragg retreated. At Chickamauga, his plans were thwarted when Polk arrived hours later than ordered. After Chickamauga, Bragg's subordinates circulated a letter urging his removal. Davis didn't help matters when he showed up at Bragg's

BRAXTON
BRAGG

1817–1876

headquarters and asked the commanders—with Bragg present—if the Army of Tennessee should have a new commander. They all said yes, but Davis postponed any action. Bragg was humiliated further at Lookout Mountain by Grant, who chased the entire Army of Tennessee down the seemingly impregnable Missionary Ridge. The disgusted Bragg asked to be relieved of command. To his surprise and displeasure, Davis accepted the resignation with haste.

The observant Civil War diarist Mary Chesnut wrote, "Bragg begs to be released from his command. The army will be relieved to get rid of him. He has a winning way of earning everybody's detestation. Heavens, how they hate him." General John Porter McCown had threatened to go home and raise potatoes on his Tennessee farm if Bragg wasn't removed from command.

The *Richmond Examiner* put it this way: "A little more *brains*, General Bragg." Another newspaper called him the man with "the iron heart, the iron hand, and the wooden head." Bragg wrote bitterly to his wife of "the venal press," particularly in Richmond, where "the dogs of detraction were let loose upon me."

Bragg was a perfect punching bag for both the press and the public—a bad-tempered man who made mistakes. The Confederacy seemed to be losing, and any scapegoat was welcome. Bragg was a favorite.

In February 1864, the ever-loyal Davis summoned Bragg to Richmond to serve as his military adviser. During eight months there, he proved a better adviser than a general. Davis and Bragg often disagreed—Bragg was not one to suck up—but Davis respected him.

In October 1864, Davis sent him to defend Wilmington, North Carolina, the last Southern port open to Confederate blockade runners. Bragg's reputation preceded him. "We suspect that General Bragg is going to Wilmington. Goodbye, Wilmington," reported the *Wilmington Journal*. The Yanks attacked nearby Fort Fisher in January 1865, and Bragg stood by several miles away wringing his hands. He never had a good explanation for why he didn't give aid to the fort's defenders.

Poor Bragg! He had an abundance of illnesses, some of them probably aggravated by stress—migraine headaches, boils, and rheumatism, among others. He wrote his wife, "I do not average four hours rest in twenty-four." Though he worked hard, it did not pay off in loyalty from those around him. The general had no ability to inspire either his officers or the men in the ranks. He divided people into friends and enemies, and he never passed up a chance to criticize a perceived enemy. He was an old friend of Joseph E. Johnston. But he was also jealous of him and was tickled pink when Johnston was replaced by Hood as commander of the Army of Tennessee. General James Longstreet complained to Davis that he was not a half-hour under Bragg's command before he "saw that General Bragg was incompetent to manage an army or put men into a fight."

Though it may have been inspired by all his problems with his generals, Bragg did make one astute comment: "History will award the main honor where it is due—to the private soldier."

Those private soldiers did not forget Bragg either. Indeed, they referred to their all-too-common body lice as "Bragg's bodyguards."

John. C. Breckinridge,
Confederate General and Politician
(1821–1875)

THE VERSATILE KENTUCKIAN

IMAGINE THIS DUTY: being a slave-owning Southerner and having to announce to Congress the election of Abraham Lincoln as president of the United States. On February 13, 1861, such was the task faced by John C. Breckinridge—vice president of the United States *and* senator from Kentucky *and* himself a presidential candidate in the 1860 election. His loss to Lincoln had propelled the Southern states into a war he knew they could not win.

His family was Kentucky aristocracy, and the tall, handsome John C. had the look of a leader. First a congressman, he was the Democratic vice president under James Buchanan at age thirty-five, the youngest vice president in United States history.

In the fateful election of 1860, he was one of four presidential candidates. (He happened to be the one supported by Buchanan, but considering "Old Buck's" unpopularity at the time, that was not much help.) At their convention, the Democrats split over the issue of slavery (a split that ultimately led to the election of the Republican, Lincoln). Breckinridge was the candidate of the Southern Democrats, who predicted, incorrectly, that the Northern Democrats' man, Stephen Douglas, would withdraw from the race. During the race, Breckinridge denied being a secessionist, yet the public identified him with Southern extremists. Oddly, he lost his home state, Kentucky, to another candidate, Constitutional Unionist John Bell, though he did carry eleven of the fifteen slave states, getting more electoral votes than either Bell or Douglas.

The weeks between Lincoln's election and inauguration were tense ones, and paranoia ran high in Washington. Rumor had it that Southerners planned to seize Washington and make Breckinridge president. Flamboyant senator Louis Wigfall of Texas suggested to John Floyd, the secretary of war, that Southerners kidnap James Buchanan and put Breckinridge in his place. The honorable John C. had nothing to do with these crackpot notions.

When the war began, Breckinridge helped formulate a neutrality policy for Kentucky. It didn't hold long. The Confederacy definitely wanted the border state (and slave state), but so did the Union.

Because Breckinridge defended the secession of the Southern states, the United States Senate expelled him. Threatened with arrest (which made no sense, since technically he had not committed treason), he fled to Virginia. Privately, he predicted that the South could not win a war against the Union.

Thanks to his name recognition and his status as a Mexican War veteran, he was commissioned a Confederate brigadier general. Breckinridge was one "political general" who actually proved a good soldier. He also helped organize the Confederate government of Kentucky, which led to the state's admission to the Confederacy. (In the interest of simplicity, historians count Kentucky as being in the Union, though the state did technically join the Confederacy and supplied it with many soldiers. It had two separate state governments, pro-Confederacy and pro-Union. Of the thirteen stars in the Confederate flag, one represented Kentucky.)

Breckinridge fought in several major battles, most notably Shiloh and Murfreesboro. Like practically everyone, he

JOHN C.
BRECKINRIDGE

1821–1875

feuded with the tactless Braxton Bragg, his commander. Friends urged him to challenge the vexatious Bragg to a duel. Later, at Chattanooga, he and Bragg again butted heads. Bragg removed Breckinridge from command after charging him with drunkenness.

In February 1864, Breckinridge (who was *not* a drunk, though he did like Kentucky bourbon) was given a new command (away from Bragg, of course) in Virginia, where he was praised for defeating the Yanks at the Battle of New Market. He was aided by cadets from the Virginia Military Institute, the heroic "Katydids," ten of whom were killed and forty-seven wounded, as any VMI graduate knows. Breckinridge uttered the famous words, "Put the boys in." Those boys' valor mightily impressed weary Rebel veterans. (The cadets' gallant charge is depicted on the walls of Jackson Memorial Hall at VMI.) Later, Breckinridge managed to keep the Yanks away from the important saltworks in southwestern Virginia.

In February 1865, Jefferson Davis appointed Breckinridge secretary of war, a revolving-door slot that was a persistent problem because Davis (a former United States secretary of war) filled that role himself. (Mary Chesnut had confided to her diary in 1861 that Breckinridge would make a fine secretary of war—far better than the "lame, tame Leroy P. Walker," the first man to fill the slot.) At the war's beginning, Breckinridge had doubted that the South could win. Four years later, he knew he was right. The best that could be done, he believed, was to wrap things up honorably. Some urged that the Confederacy carry on the war using no-holds-barred guerrilla tactics, but the highborn Breckinridge would have none of it. The war, he said, was "a magnificent epic. In God's name let it not terminate in a farce."

In his role as secretary of war, Breckinridge was at Joe Johnston's side when he surrendered his armies to Sherman in North Carolina. Having gone days without a taste of liquor, the bourbon drinker was pleased that Sherman offered him one. But he was immensely peeved when Sherman later took a drink without offering to share. He subsequently told Johnston that Sherman was "a hog" and that "no Kentucky gentleman would have taken away that bottle. He knew we needed it, and badly."

Breckinridge made his way to Canada and remained in exile until Andrew Johnson issued his general amnesty for Confederates. He returned to practice law in Kentucky, calling himself an "extinct volcano." He died at age fifty-four.

Mary Chesnut wrote perceptively, "Nothing narrow, nothing self-seeking about Breckinridge."

John Brown, Abolitionist
(1800–1859)

MANIAC MARTYR

WAS HE A HOLY martyr or a crackpot? The Connecticut-born abolitionist agitator is one of the more controversial figures in United States history. One glimpse at a picture of the stern, craggy-faced John Brown will convince you that this was not a politician or a peacemaker. Brown had one driving motivation in life: Free the slaves. God willed it. That was all there was to it.

It was appropriate that the rough-hewn Brown was born in New England. Most of his support—moral and financial—came from there. Most New Englanders had long since thrown aside their ancestors' Calvinistic Christianity, but they were still Puritans at heart. They wanted a cause, and they wanted to purify the land. Brown became their darling. He was a friend (so he told them) of the weak and oppressed. Most of his New England supporters had never rubbed shoulders with slaves or slave owners, but what did it matter? Brown seemed sincere, and zealous to boot, and if he and his followers slaughtered some proslavery people in Kansas, that was God's will, as Brown said. The East Coast abolitionists overlooked the fact that Brown's band dragged unarmed people from their beds and hacked them up with swords.

Brown's God was the Old Testament deity, vengeful and violent, not the peace-loving, turn-the-other-cheek God of the New Testament. Brown thought the Old Testament and a sword were the Lord's instruments for stamping out sin. He could drop words like *bullets* and *bayonets* and *God's will* in the same sentence. And he had no patience with "gradual" emancipationists. To one of them, he shouted, "Caution, sir? I am eternally tired of hearing that word, *caution*. It is nothing but the word of cowardice!"

Brown showed no caution whatsoever in his antislavery killing sprees. He and his followers were key reasons why the nickname "Bleeding Kansas" came into being in the 1850s. Up for grabs between proslavery and antislavery settlers, Kansas was the scene of the Pottawatomie Massacre in May 1856.

Brown and his gang slaughtered a number of proslavery settlers. His band hacked a farmer named Doyle and his sons to death. One boy had his head sliced open and both arms cut off. Brown shot Doyle square in the forehead. This Brown was the man proper Bostonians adored as an angel of righteousness.

The abolitionist saint then concocted a ludicrous plan to free slaves throughout the South. It had as much chance as a snowball in Key West, but Brown, like all good fanatics, was not deterred by reality. In October 1859, he made a place for himself in the history books by using an "army" of twenty-one men to raid the federal armory at Harpers Ferry, Virginia, hoping to arm slaves with the weapons. United States Marines (under the command of a colonel named Robert E. Lee) nipped the plan in the bud. (The shortsighted Brown had not even attempted to spread word of the raid to slaves in the area.) Two of Brown's sons were killed, and old John himself was wounded.

He was tried for treason and went calmly to his death by hanging. His last remark was that the Virginia countryside was quite pretty. Present at the hanging was a young military professor named Thomas Jackson (who has gone down in history as "Stonewall"). Another spectator present was named John Wilkes Booth.

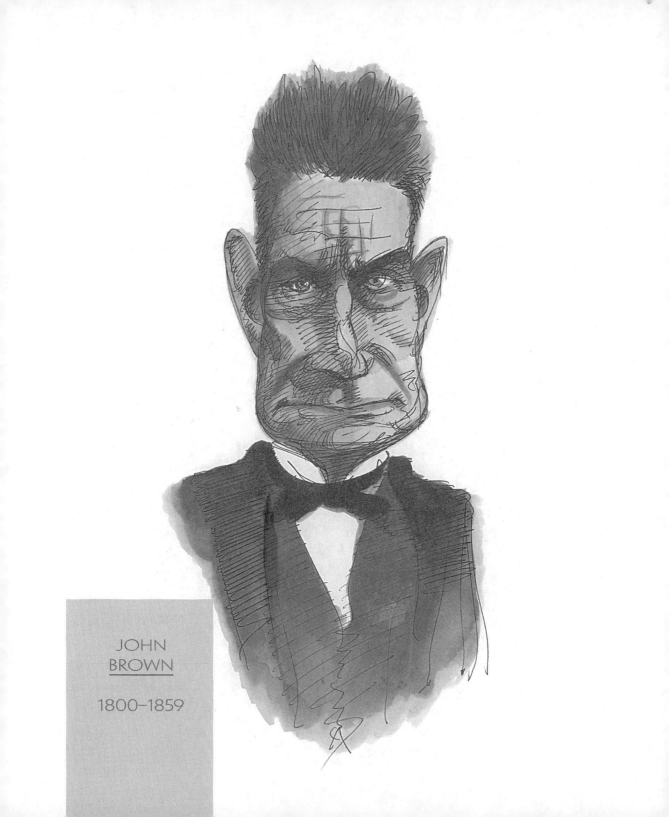

JOHN
BROWN

1800–1859

Brown's trial unearthed some interesting facts. Many of his ancestors had been mentally ill, and he himself (surprise!) had shown signs of such illness. But Brown refused to plead insanity.

If Brown was insane, there was a method to his madness. He undoubtedly *wanted* to be a martyr (since he'd had no other success in life), and he undoubtedly knew that his actions at Harpers Ferry would result in his arrest and execution. (To say that Brown failed at everything except becoming a martyr doesn't quite do him justice. He did succeed at one other thing: fathering children. To be specific, twenty children by two different wives.)

Brown also knew how the antislavery crowd would react. Abolitionists were ecstatic; they had a martyr. The poet Henry Wadsworth Longfellow was typical of Yankee intellectuals. He wrote in his diary that Brown's execution was "the date of a new revolution, quite as much needed as the old one." Henry David Thoreau called Brown "this Angel of Light." Never mind that many Northern clergymen and politicians—including Abraham Lincoln and Stephen Douglas—denounced Brown as a cold-hearted murderer who deserved to die.

For their part, Southerners heard only the voices of the exultant abolitionists. Southerners were enraged—and scared. They feared that someone more organized and more levelheaded than Brown would attempt the same kind of thing—and succeed.

Brown's death thus became the "wedge" issue of the day. In some ways, his Harpers Ferry raid was the first battle of the Civil War.

The great hero of the antislavery crowd was immortalized in the lyrics, "John Brown's body lies a-moldering in the grave; His soul goes marching on." The tune proved more durable than the words. We still sing the "Battle Hymn of the Republic" to it.

Brown was buried, appropriately, in a black community in North Elba, New York, a community founded on land donated by a fellow abolitionist.

William G. Brownlow, Pro-Union Journalist and Governor
(1805–1877)

PRICKLY PARSON

PARSON BROWNLOW had much in common with his fellow Tennessean Andrew Johnson: both opposed secession, both were strong on the Union, and (surprise!) neither was opposed to slavery. Both men served as governors of Union-occupied Tennessee. And like Johnson, Brownlow was often the center of controversy. But

Brownlow seemed to actually relish it.

Brownlow was known as "Parson" because he had been a Methodist circuit-riding preacher in his younger days. As such, he never seemed to have much concern for the fruits of the Spirit (love, for example), for the main theme of his preaching was the errors of other denominations (a favorite sermon topic in those days). Happily for Christianity, Brownlow turned to another career, mostly because he couldn't support his growing family on the salary of a contentious preacher. He became a journalist, a fertile field for a man with a pen warmed up in hell.

His paper, the *Knoxville Whig*, had a wide circulation and an even wider reputation for being as opinionated and mean-spirited as its editor. Brownlow declared that he would "fight the secessionist leaders till hell froze over." While spewing out his anti-secession views, he still found time to author venomous books against Catholics, Baptists, Presbyterians, immigrants, and (his unpardonable sin in the eyes of most Southerners) the Democratic Party.

Though he was proslavery (a white supremacist, in fact), "the Fighting Parson" had no time for secession. "I am for the Union though every other institution in the country perish," he wrote. He once confronted secession advocate William L. Yancey, telling him that all secessionists should be skewered with bayonets. (Yancey, every bit as scrappy and caustic as Brownlow, said he would gladly plunge a bayonet in Brownlow's heart.)

Brownlow was one of many pro-Union stalwarts in Tennessee's mountainous eastern counties. The region had few slaves, and most of its residents resented the political power wielded by the wealthy plantation lords of Middle and West Tennessee. Once Tennessee seceded, Brownlow and his fellow Unionists tried (but failed) to make East Tennessee a separate state. Such efforts had worked with the western counties of Virginia (which became the new state of West Virginia during the war), but there was one crucial difference in Tennessee: the east was under the firm control of the Confederates. Also, the Tennessee legislature was not keen on the idea.

For much of the war, the Fighting Parson played the role of the Confederacy's chief critic in Tennessee. He defiantly flew the Union flag over his home. His position as publisher of the only openly pro-Union paper in the Confederacy made his life chancy, and he loved every minute of it.

But a new nation fighting for its life could not long tolerate such a critic—or *traitor*, as the South saw him. Brownlow swore he would rather be in prison than pledge loyalty to the Confederacy. He was no doubt pleased when the Confederacy ordered his arrest for treason. Not all Confederates were willing to await his trial; they wrecked his presses.

Anti-Brownlow feeling grew when some of his fellow Unionists burned vital bridges in East Tennessee. Some of the suspects were

WILLIAM G.
BROWNLOW

1805–1877

hanged, their bodies left in public for days as a warning to potential traitors. Brownlow denied any connection, but the Rebels were (for good reason) highly suspicious.

To his relief, the Confederacy allowed him to cross to Union-occupied territory in March 1862. Jefferson Davis's administration had decided, wisely, that it didn't want to transform Brownlow into a martyr for freedom of the press. Brownlow had declared he would rather live in prison than in the Confederacy anyway.

After his release, Brownlow continued his mission as a pro-Union, anti-South propaganda machine. He went on a highly successful speaking tour in the North, railing against the South and relishing his role as an exiled patriot. *Parson Brownlow's Book* (its full title was *Sketches of the Rise, Progress, and Decline of Secession*) became a bestseller.

When the Federals occupied Knoxville, he returned to Tennessee and began publishing a paper with the catchy title of *Knoxville Whig and Rebel Ventilator*. His pro-Union stance finally paid off. In January 1865, he was elected governor of Tennessee (an election in which, of course, only Union men voted). He replaced Andrew Johnson, who had been elected vice president, and who would be president sooner than anyone knew. In fact, Brownlow became governor ten days after Johnson became president.

Brownlow continued in that office after the war ended. He took great pleasure in imposing the "damnesty oath," which barred former Confederates from voting. He pushed the legislature to declare Tennessee's Confederate governor, Isham Harris, guilty of treason and to issue a warrant for his arrest. The Fighting Parson was in the governor's chair when Tennessee became the first Confederate state readmitted to the Union.

The parson with the poison pen had always described himself as a "national man." Appropriately enough, he went to Washington as one of Tennessee's senators in 1869.

Simon Bolivar Buckner, Confederate General
(1823–1914)

GRANT'S OCCASIONAL FRIEND

SIMON BOLIVAR, the South American freedom fighter known as "the Liberator," was widely admired in the United States, and this Confederate was one of many sons named in his honor.

Buckner was a Kentucky boy, a West Point graduate (he won the saber championship there), and, like so many Civil War generals, a Mexican War veteran. He owned no slaves and hoped Kentucky would remain neutral when the war erupted. That was the pipe dream (though a noble one) of the state's governor, who had the improbable name of Beriah Magoffin. The governor had Southern sympathies and allowed Confederate recruiters to operate in the state. But he genuinely wanted it neutral, probably hoping that if Kentucky stayed out of the fight, his political future would be solid no matter which side won.

On the grounds of being neutral, Buckner refused a commission in the United States army *and* the Confederate army. What prompted his shift from neutrality was the order issued by Kentucky's Unionist-dominated legislature to expel all Confederate troops from the state. Buckner, head of the Kentucky militia, responded by asking Kentuckians to "defend their homes against the invasion of the North." Under suspicion of being a traitor, he fled south, where the new Confederate government made him a brigadier general. Much of the Kentucky militia, being pro-Southern, went with him, a package deal that pleased the Confederates. Buckner served under another gallant Kentuckian, Albert Sidney Johnston.

In February 1862 came a confrontation that was surely the most memorable of his Civil War service.

One of Buckner's West Point chums was U. S. Grant. Between West Point and the Civil War, Buckner encountered a boozy, depressed (and broke) Grant living in a dingy hotel called the What Cheer House. Buckner gave his old buddy money to pay for his hotel room.

They met again in Tennessee in 1862, when Grant (of whom little was expected in those days) advanced on Forts Henry and Donelson. The two forts—Henry on the Tennessee River, Donelson on the Cumberland River—were only eleven miles apart. They guarded the water routes into Kentucky, Tennessee, and northern Alabama and were, as Grant knew, a gateway to the mid-South.

Grant took Fort Henry without much resistance, and he expected little from Donelson, for he knew its commander, General John Floyd, and Floyd's second in command, Gideon Pillow, both political generals. When Grant was on the verge of capturing Fort Donelson, Floyd chose to flee, passing on the command to Pillow, who opted to flee, passing on the command to . . . Simon Bolivar Buckner. The passing of the buck was accomplished with quick formality.

Floyd: "I turn over the command."

Pillow: "I pass it."

Buckner: "I accept it."

Buckner remarked to Pillow that the commanders clearly preferred their feather beds to the hard planks of a prison camp. No doubt disgusted with those two incompetent old men, Buckner kindly advised his troops, "It was not your fault, my brave boys, it was not your fault."

SIMON
BOLIVAR
BUCKNER

1823–1914

Gritty cavalry commander Nathan Bedford Forrest stamped off in disgust: "I did not come here to surrender my command!" Before the surrender, he led his cavalrymen away through the frozen Tennessee landscape littered with soldiers' corpses.

Buckner, the third banana now elevated to top banana, sent a message to Grant requesting a discussion to lay out terms for surrendering the fort. Grant gained his famous nickname when he demanded "no terms except unconditional and immediate surrender." Grudgingly (and no doubt peeved that his past kindness was cutting no ice with Grant), Buckner returned a message that conditions "compel me to accept the ungenerous and unchivalrous terms which you propose."

U. S. "Unconditional Surrender" Grant was pleasant at their meeting (and why not, since he was the winner?). They swapped a few reminiscences, and Grant admitted that taking Fort Donelson would have been harder had Buckner himself been in charge.

Buckner was shipped off to grim Fort Warren prison in Massachusetts but was soon exchanged. Rather than being censured by the Confederates for surrendering Donelson, he was promoted to major general. Back in the saddle again, he proved himself a competent commander in Tennessee, although he locked

horns (as all generals inevitably did) with temperamental, fractious Braxton Bragg. Buckner was one of the group of disgruntled generals who petitioned the Confederate government to sack Bragg.

The last major Confederate army surrendered to the Union on May 26, 1865, several weeks after Appomattox. Its commanding general was Simon Bolivar Buckner. The triumphant Union restricted him to Louisiana for a while, but he returned home to Kentucky in 1868 and became a wealthy and influential businessman. He was elected governor in 1887.

Besides the tragicomic episode at Fort Donelson, Buckner is remembered as the first commander of the famous "Orphan Brigade" (First Kentucky Brigade), which took its nickname from being "orphaned" by its home state. Though split between pro-Confederate and pro-Union factions, Kentucky stayed in Union hands throughout the war, and the First Kentucky had to train in Tennessee. It fought in some of the major battles in Tennessee and Georgia. Unable to recruit new men on its home turf, it dwindled from its original four thousand soldiers to about five hundred. Nonetheless, the unit was one of the best in the entire Army of Tennessee, according to many generals. One of its generals was Ben

Hardin Helm, brother-in-law of Mary Lincoln.

Buckner died at the ripe old age of ninety, having lived long enough to more than balance out his four less-than-blissful Rebel years.

The Buckner name ended up in an unlikely place: Okinawa. World War II general Simon Bolivar Buckner, Jr., was killed in action there in 1945. A bay at Okinawa is called Buckner Bay in his honor.

Ambrose E. Burnside, Union General
(1824–1881)

MR. NICE GUY, OUT OF HIS DEPTH

IF NAME RECOGNITION counts for anything, Ambrose Burnside remains the most-often-referred-to Civil War general. His distinctive style of facial hair passed into the language as *sideburns*—a slight variation of his name. It is well that his facial hair is remembered, because he wasn't a particularly good general. But then, he never claimed to be, which set him apart from the blaring egos that surrounded him.

Burnside was born in a log cabin, one of nine sons of a former South Carolinian who moved to Indiana after freeing his slaves. His many siblings knew him as

"Brose." He went to West Point, where in one year, he accumulated 198 demerits, just 2 short of dismissal.

But he was popular. A fellow officer said Burnside was a man whose "sincerity, frankness, and amiability of manner made everybody like him." He was a night person, chatting and playing cards till past midnight, then catching up on letter writing till dawn.

Mr. Nice Guy was (like most Civil War generals) a Mexican War veteran. He resigned from the army in 1853 to open a factory to produce a rifle of his own design, the "Burnside carbine." The government contract he counted on never came, and he was forced to declare bankruptcy. During the war, more than fifty-five thousand Burnside carbines were produced, but creditors controlled his patents, so Burnside earned not a penny. The poor man was also stood up at the altar by a flighty Kentucky belle, Charlotte "Lottie" Moon. The story goes that at the point in the ceremony where she was asked if she would take Ambrose as her husband, she snapped, "No, siree, Bob, I won't," then stomped out.

The war returned Burnside to military life. At First Manassas, he commanded a brigade and was made a brigadier general by an admiring Lincoln. His next theater of activity was North Carolina, where he led the Union armada of fifteen thousand men and eighty ships that captured Roanoke Island (which was defended by only fifteen hundred men), then New Bern, Beaufort, and Fort Macon. For this, he was promoted to major general in March 1862. Union spirits had sagged since First Manassas, so his capture of Roanoke Island was a great boost to morale and a bitter pill for the South to swallow.

Bad luck followed good. At the hellish Battle of Antietam in Maryland, Burnside's determination to get his troops across a defended bridge over Antietam Creek—the infamous "Burnside Bridge"—delayed his arrival on the field. It was a permanent smudge on his record.

Unlike egotists such as George McClellan, Burnside had doubts about his ability as a commander. As Lincoln became disillusioned with McClellan's dallying, he twice offered Burnside command of the Army of the Potomac. Twice, Burnside declined. He finally accepted the assignment in November 1862. After traveling through a blinding snowstorm, he delivered (with no pleasure) Lincoln's message relieving McClellan of command. He told the generals under him that he knew he was "not fit for so big a command" but would do his best.

His best wasn't very good, or very wise. Burnside decided to attack Lee's army at

AMBROSE E.
BURNSIDE

1824–1881

Fredericksburg, Virginia, midway between Washington and Richmond, then march on to Richmond. He foolishly declared that the enemy was "weakened" and that with "the help of Providence we would be able to strike a death blow to the Rebellion." Providence didn't help—not the Yanks, anyway. From Marye's Heights, Rebel lead rained down on the pitiful Union troops. The Union army suffered 12,700 dead. Burnside lost the battle and Lincoln's confidence, and the Northern army's morale flagged.

More bad luck: the infamous "Mud March." Attempting to cross the Rappahannock River in January 1863, Burnside did not reckon with his demoralized army's need for rest. A driving rain and high winds set in for forty-eight hours. The roads clogged with vehicles, artillery, horses, and mules, all mired in mud. Burnside finally admitted the situation was hopeless and ordered the troops back to their old camp. Two days later, he was replaced by Joseph Hooker, one of the few people the warm-hearted Burnside sincerely disliked.

More tough luck: At Petersburg, Virginia, in the spring of 1864, Burnside watched as his men were slaughtered at the Battle of the Crater. The plan was to use soldiers who were Pennsylvania coal miners to dig a tunnel under the Confederate fortifications. The Yanks would then blow up the Rebels, and Union troops would pour in through the breach. When the mine was detonated, it produced an immense volume of debris, smoke, and flame. So far so good, but the Union men who entered the newly formed crater soon found themselves easy targets and struggled wildly to escape. Grenades were thrown in by the Confederates, and heads, arms, and legs sailed through the air. For improper handling of troops, Burnside was relieved of command. He resigned his commission on April 15, 1865—the day Lincoln died.

Burnside's Bridge, Marye's Heights, the Mud March, the Crater—there were several bloody blots on the man's record. Fortunately, fate was kinder to the good-humored Burnside after the war. He was three times elected governor of Rhode Island. In 1874, he was elected to the Senate, where he served until his death.

Regarding Lottie Moon, the belle who jilted him: she and her sister Ginnie both became notorious Confederate spies. When Ginnie ran afoul of Federal authorities, Lottie prevailed upon General Burnside, her almost-husband, to help her sister out of a tough spot. He did. Good-hearted, wasn't he? Ginnie lived long enough to become a Hollywood actress, and Lottie became a Baptist missionary.

Benjamin Franklin Butler, Union General

(1818–1893)

THE NASTY OF N'AWLINS

LEGEND HAS IT that some New Orleans residents had pictures of Beast painted on the bottoms of their chamber pots. Everyone in the Confederacy knew who Beast was: the loathsome, potbellied, cross-eyed Massachusetts politician who governed Union-occupied New Orleans. Diarist Mary Chesnut referred to him as "this hideous cross-eyed beast."

Funny that Butler became the Yankee bogeyman, because during the 1860 Democratic Convention, it was he who nominated Jefferson Davis for president. In fact, Beast was a proslavery Democrat who campaigned for John Breckinridge, the South's Democratic candidate in the race. But once the Civil War began, the Beast was raring to kiss up to Lincoln, the Republican president.

Beast Butler was one of the Union's political generals. Back home in Massachusetts, he was a political force and a successful (and none too scrupulous) criminal lawyer. He was also rather bluntly anti-Semitic, claiming that King John of England knew how to deal with Jews: "fry them in swine's fat."

Like most political generals, Butler loved the "show" of soldiering. He had a gorgeous uniform bedecked with rich gold embroidery. One observer noted that he "looked around with a sort of triumphant gaze, as if to assure himself that the bystanders were duly impressed." He was once described as a politician "who could strut sitting down." Why did Lincoln keep him in uniform? Because Butler was a big man among Northern Democrats.

He also had some smarts. Butler concocted the plan to seize New Orleans and close the Mississippi to Confederate trade. It was a brilliant idea, and his reward was the post of military governor of the occupied city. The loss of the Crescent City was a severe blow to Southern morale and a cause for rejoicing in the North.

But Butler's behavior as governor led to his infamous nickname. An actor on a political stage, he felt he had to show how pro-Union he was. One of his first acts was to execute William Mumford, a professional gambler, for cutting down a Union flag. The proud New Orleans women were a problem, too. They mouthed off to Union soldiers, spat on the Union flag, and stepped off the sidewalks rather than pass a Yankee. One woman emptied her slop jar on the head of Union naval hero David Farragut as he passed under her balcony. To Beast's never-ending infamy, he issued the notorious "Woman's Order" of May 15, 1862. In brief, it stated that any woman insulting a Yankee soldier would be treated as a common streetwalker.

General Beauregard, proud Louisiana aristocrat that he was, issued a righteous response to Butler's order: "Men of the South! Shall our mothers, our wives, our daughters, and our sisters, be thus outraged by the ruffianly soldiers of the North, to whom is given the right to treat, at their pleasure, the ladies of the South as common harlots? Arouse, friends, and drive back from our soil those infamous invaders."

President Jefferson Davis, chivalrous to the bone, issued a proclamation that Butler, "a felon, an outlaw, a common enemy of mankind," would, if captured, be hanged immediately.

The outcry went beyond America. Britain's prime minister, Lord Palmerston, called Butler's order "infamous" (a curious criticism, considering what a womanizer Palmerston was).

Beast had one woman arrested for laughing

BENJAMIN
FRANKLIN
BUTLER

1818–1893

as a Yankee funeral procession passed by. He imprisoned Mayor Monroe (who had made his anti-Yankee sentiments known) for the duration of the war. Rumor had it that he filched family silver while in residence in town, so in addition to being known as "Beast Butler," he was also "Spoons Butler." To the dismay of the booze-loving city, Beast ordered breweries and distilleries closed. He took New Orleans church bells that the Confederates planned to melt into cannon and sold them at auction in Boston. Mary Chesnut wrote of Beast, "We hardly expected from Massachusetts behavior to shame a Comanche." Butler's rule in New Orleans was a regular propaganda mill for the South.

Beast grew paranoid in the city that hated him. Foreign consuls complained that Butler treated them as if they were Confederate agents. In turn, European governments complained to Washington about Butler's treatment of their representatives. So Lincoln had a political reason for removing Butler. He had a military reason as well: he knew Butler would be a poor field commander in the proposed expedition up the Mississippi. Butler was removed from New Orleans in December 1862.

Lincoln later gave Butler a curious order. Beast was to go back to Louisiana and raise an army from the slaves soon to be freed by the Emancipation Proclamation. Butler had no desire to be a recruiting agent; he wanted his former command back. But Lincoln had no intention of giving Butler another field command—ever.

In 1864, it was by no means inevitable that Lincoln would be renominated. Butler, now a Republican, and still greedy for power, made himself available. It was suggested that he serve as running mate for Salmon P. Chase, Lincoln's less-than-loyal secretary of the treasury. Butler said maybe to this, but boasted that since he might yet capture Richmond, he would of course run for president, not vice president. He bragged that he could take an army within thirty miles of Richmond without any trouble (which was laughable, coming from such an inept general). As it turned out, Lincoln won reelection easily.

Butler did run for president—in 1884, as the candidate of the Greenback Party. He got 1.74 percent of the popular vote and no electoral votes.

Simon Cameron, Union Politician
(1799–1889)

THE CRAFT OF GRAFT

SHAKESPEARE WROTE, "The devil hath power t'assume a pleasing shape," and the Bible tells us that Satan "masquerades as an angel of light." But fortunately for the human race, some devious and corrupt people really *look* devious and corrupt. Simon Cameron did. And in that pre-video age, he didn't care that he did. He was something rare today, a politician who made little effort to cultivate an "Honest John" image. Cameron was a party man, a man whose most-quoted words (which, incidentally, best applied to him) defined a good politician as one who "when he's bought, *stays* bought."

How did the "Czar of Pennsylvania" end up in the cabinet of Lincoln? As a loyal Republican Party man, and in return for giving Pennsylvania's electoral votes to Lincoln, he was made (with great reluctance) the new president's secretary of war. Lincoln supposedly said, "How can I justify my title of Honest Abe with the appointment of a man like Cameron?"

Cameron himself had presidential aspirations. At the 1860 Republican Convention, Pennsylvania's delegates were Cameron's men. But Cameron let Lincoln know he would have the delegates vote for Lincoln if Lincoln made him secretary of the treasury. Lincoln was unwilling to strike that bargain, but his campaign managers were. So, after his election, he owed Cameron a favor.

Cameron's enemies (and he had many) tried to convince Lincoln that Cameron was "the very incarnation of corruption" and had acquired his fortune "by means forbidden to the man of honor." If he was corrupt—and he definitely was—there was yet something to admire in the snake. He was a self-made tycoon, an orphan boy who began as a typesetter at age ten, then became a printer, then editor of his own newspaper at age twenty-one. Getting a state contract for printing whet his appetite for government money. Soaking up both private and public dollars, he made a fortune in banking, railroads, and canal building.

Lincoln gave him the War Department instead of the Treasury Department, because putting Cameron in charge of Federal finances seemed too cruel a joke to play on the country.

In a nation poised for war, Cameron faced a daunting task. Simply put, the best officers in the United States Army were heading south. Cameron stated that "without this startling defection, the Rebellion never could have assumed formidable proportions." A total of 228 graduates of West Point departed for the Confederacy. Another 159 officers not trained at West Point also joined the army of the new nation. How did this happen?

Partly to blame was a previous secretary of war, Jefferson Davis, who served under Franklin Pierce. There is little doubt that while he was secretary of war, Davis was training a Southern cadre of first-class military men in case secession ever came to pass. Consider the list of field officers in the Second Cavalry Regiment, organized by Davis: Robert E. Lee, Albert Sidney Johnston, William J. Hardee, Earl Van Dorn, Edmund Kirby Smith, John B. Hood, Fitzhugh Lee, all of whom became Confederate notables. When the war began, Davis's policy of favoring Southern men—a policy that Winfield Scott, a Virginian, abetted—paid off. The North began the war with

SIMON
CAMERON

1799–1889

a severe lack of trained leaders. The pool of talent was barely a mud puddle. Now that he was president of the Confederacy, Davis was no doubt pleased with his work as secretary of war.

As if that weren't bad enough, Cameron was intent on lining his pockets with bribes. During his (fortunately brief) tenure as secretary of war, there were reports of graft and corruption—contracts going to the highest bidder, spoiled meat, shoddy clothing, guns that would either not fire or would harm the shooter more than the target. As one Union supporter claimed, "You can sell anything to the government at almost any price you've got the guts to ask." General Sherman (who hated politicians in general) complained that "in this time of trial, cheating in clothes, blankets, flour, bread, everything, is universal."

The Senate insisted that Cameron supply a detailed report on contracts—the amounts, names of contractors, dates, payments, etc. Cameron ignored the request. He also dispensed political favors and offices to Pennsylvania men and family members. The Republicans generally let Cameron be, since he was one of them—that is, he was antislavery. To gratify the party, he included in his annual report a long memo on the evils of slavery.

He stroked the Republicans further by proclaiming that the Union should enlist black troops. And strictly speaking, there was no hard evidence against him. *Technically*, he had committed no crime.

Lincoln was in a pickle. In a nation at war, the most corrupt man in his administration was the secretary of war. He figured a way out: he made Cameron ambassador to Russia, a sort of banishment. The Czar of Pennsylvania was sent to the Czar of Russia. One senator who knew of Cameron's dishonesty stated that the government should "send word to the Czar to bring in his things at night." Cameron wasn't long in Russia before he decided to return to the United States Senate. Lincoln's new secretary of war was the ill-tempered, paranoid (but also efficient and honest) Edwin Stanton.

Corrupt living sometimes brings long life. Cameron died at age ninety. And he lived on genetically; for the next twenty years, the political machine he had run was managed by his son.

Simon Cameron's place in history is assured not because he served briefly in Lincoln's cabinet, but because he was one of the most powerful political bosses the United States has ever seen.

Salmon P. Chase, Union Politician
(1808–1873)

THE MAN WHO WOULD BE CREAM

"BE SATISFIED WITH SKIM MILK when you can't get cream." So said Chase when he was an Ohio lawyer. After years of frustration when he ached to be United States president (the cream), he was appointed the Supreme Court's chief justice (the skim milk).

Chase was like many ambitious men— his home life was unhappy. In a period of seventeen years, he stood at the caskets of three wives and four children. His chief consolation was his beloved daughter Kate, who played chess with him, talked politics, and was, some said, as much a son as a daughter could be. She became his Washington hostess, and her 1863 wedding was

Washington's grandest social event during the war years. She despised Lincoln and probably increased her father's own disdain for the man who made him treasury secretary and later chief justice.

Chase and Lincoln were both Republicans but had little else in common. Chase was more brazenly antislavery than Lincoln, which probably kept him from the presidential nomination he burned for. His abolitionism was sincere. In his early years lawyering in Cincinnati, he handled (without fee) the cases of fugitive slaves. (Indeed, Kentuckians across the river called him the "attorney general for runaway Negroes.") He was sometimes persecuted for his antislavery views; once, while speaking, he was hit with a brick and rotten eggs. To his credit, he wasn't in it for the money. Lawyering for runaway slaves did not pay as well as corporate law would have.

The man impressed. One witness described Chase as "tall, broad-shouldered, and proudly erect . . . a picture of intelligence, strength, courage, and dignity." He was twice voted governor of Ohio, then United States senator. But these were mere steppingstones. Rumor had it that he was in the habit of standing before a mirror, bowing to himself, and saying, "President Chase." But the folksy Lincoln won the 1860 Republican nomination,

though Chase was a serious contender. Ambition counts for something, but luck and timing are always factors.

So Lincoln was president, and several Southern states left the Union. Chase's reaction? In early 1861, he reportedly told a newspaper editor that the only thing left to do was "call a convention of the people and let them decide how the Union was to be divided." The citizens should then "adopt the plan of recognizing secession as a right." Considering this good-riddance view, it is amazing that Lincoln had any place for Chase in his administration.

In fact, the appointment came with no great conviction on either side. The newly elected Lincoln called in Chase (who had just been elected senator) and said he "wasn't exactly prepared" to offer him the post of treasury secretary, but would he accept it if offered? Chase wouldn't promise but said he would think it over. He ultimately accepted, mostly as a way of keeping his presidential options open.

As secretary of the treasury, Chase had about as much grasp of finance as Lincoln had, which was nearly zero. Mr. Ambition could not take his mind off the presidency. The war dragged on, and Lincoln's popularity rose and fell with the Union's military successes and failures. Chase, like everyone else in the cabi-

SALMON P.
CHASE

1808–1873

net, was frustrated with General George McClellan, who promised everything and did nothing. Chase said that were *he* president, McClellan would be shot, not just removed from command. In a letter to Lincoln, Chase said that "either the government or McClellan must go down."

The treasury post did not keep Chase busy enough. In hundreds of letters to politicians and newspaper editors, he undermined confidence in Lincoln by giving the impression that he, Chase, was the one competent man in an administration of buffoons. He touted his "respect and affection" for Abe at the same time he wrote, "I think a man of different qualities from those of the President will be needed for the next four years." The infamous "Pomeroy Circular" was a pro-Chase, anti-Lincoln letter from the office of Kansas senator Samuel Pomeroy. When newspapers printed it, Chase was mortified. The kindhearted Abe absolved Chase of any part in the matter.

Chase was heartsick that his home state, Ohio, came out strongly for Lincoln in 1864. So did the Union at large, and Lincoln was reelected. He charitably overlooked Chase's backstabbing and ambition.

But he wouldn't overlook incompetence.

Lincoln had no taste for the intricacies of finance. He knew only that Chase was earning a reputation as a bad treasury secretary. More than once, Chase sent a message to Lincoln: "I respectfully resign." (For his part, Lincoln was never sure how respectful Chase was.) At the fourth resignation, Abe accepted. He replaced the soft-money Chase with a hard-money man, William P. Fessenden, though he hardly knew the difference himself.

On the death of Chief Justice Roger Taney, Lincoln (under pressure from pushy senator Charles Sumner) appointed Chase to succeed him on the Supreme Court. He did so grudgingly, telling a friend he "would rather have swallowed this buckhorn chair than to have nominated Chase." But Lincoln told someone else, "Chase is, on the whole, a pretty good fellow. His only trouble is that he has 'the White House fever' a little too bad, but I hope this may cure him and that he will be satisfied."

In December 1864, Chase was sworn in as chief justice. He found that the skim milk was not so bad. In March 1865, he swore in Lincoln at his second inauguration. In April, following Lincoln's assassination, he swore in the new president, Andrew Johnson.

George Armstrong Custer, Union General
(1839–1876)

THE PRETTINESS OF GLORY

CUSTER WILL ALWAYS be remembered for his death at the hands of the Sioux at Little Bighorn, but long before "Custer's Last Stand," the general was nationally famous as a Union hero of the Civil War. He intended it that way, and had it not been for the Sioux's killing of the one they called "Long Hair," he might have had a longer and even more splendid career. But just as in the old Greek tragedies, the too-proud hero was cut down in his prime.

He never went by the name George, but was always Armstrong or, to those close to him, "Autie," which was how his infant tongue mangled the name Armstrong. He was a blacksmith's son; his father called the young Custer his "yellow-haired laddie." Autie ached to be a soldier, but his appointment to West Point seems to have come about because his girlfriend's father (who detested him) pulled strings to get the young man away from his daughter. It worked.

Custer was first in his West Point class—first from the bottom, that is. Last, in other words. (He shared this distinction with an earlier West Point man, Confederate general George Pickett.) Custer's West Point mates dubbed him "Fanny" for his blond hair and fair skin, and they loved the mischief maker who barely scraped through academically.

He graduated in a fateful year: 1861. Specifically, he graduated ten days before First Manassas. The glory-craving Custer wasn't about to miss the chance to shine. He was at First Manassas as a lieutenant. By war's end, he was a major general. In fact, he moved from captain to brigadier general in only five months. He was blunt about his goals: "My every thought was ambitious—not to be wealthy, not to be learned, but to be great . . . not only to the present but to future generations."

Custer—his German family's name was originally Küster—was the North's counterpart to the South's Jeb Stuart. He was a pretty, dashing, fearless cavalry man with gilded spurs that jingle-jangled. His uniform was one of a

kind: black velvet trimmed in gold lace, his trademark red silk necktie (which the men of his Michigan brigade adopted as their insignia), a wide-brimmed black felt hat with a gold cord. With his gold ringlets flying and his necktie blaring like a trumpet, Custer cut quite a figure. And it wasn't just prettiness. The man had an audacity (his critics said stupidity) in battle that wouldn't permit him to stop for minor inconveniences like having eleven horses shot from under him. (He was luckier than his mounts, being wounded only once.) He became, at age twenty-three, the youngest Union general. Some of the men called him "the Boy General of the Golden Locks." The senior generals marked him as a comer. His admirers called him gutsy. His enemies (and such vain men create many) called him stupid and rash.

Playing the role of the *beau galant* required Custer to be chivalrous as well as beautiful and brave. When the Federals entered Charlottesville, Virginia, he issued orders against looting. He treated one local planter's family so well that they didn't get to spew out all the anti-Yankee sarcasm they had planned. But one of the girls, finding on the floor a silver spoon belonging to the family, asked Custer if it had fallen out of his pocket. (The looting of family silver was a common theme

GEORGE
ARMSTRONG
CUSTER

1839–1876

in stories of Union occupation. Families hid it in outhouses, in smokehouses, in the cribs of sleeping babies, under the bedcovers of pregnant women and ailing old ladies, under barn floors, inside chimneys, even in birds' nests.)

Whatever Southerners thought of Custer, his men idolized him. He idolized himself, too. His letters to his wife were not an exercise in modesty: "Oh, could you but have seen some of the charges that were made! While thinking of them I cannot but exclaim, 'Glorious War!'" Yet like all noble knights, Custer was both a lover *and* a fighter. He wrote his wife, "While I am still as strongly wedded to the 'noble profession of arms' as I ever have been, I frequently discover myself acting as umpire between my patriotism and my desire to be and remain with my darling."

Touching, isn't it? In fact, his courtship of the devout and beautiful Libbie Bacon was one of the great romances of the war. Their letters read like an 1860s version of the Song of Solomon. When some of Autie's belongings were captured by the Rebels, a Richmond newspaper published Libbie's letters to her beloved. After that, he cautioned her that "somebody must be more careful hereafter in the use of double entendres." There was heat as well as warmth in their marriage.

Apparently, the war was not big enough for both Custer and Jeb Stuart. The renowned Stuart was killed north of Richmond in a cavalry charge led by Custer. But Custer faced another formidable Rebel on horseback, the partisan leader John Mosby, the "Gray Ghost." Mosby's swift-moving guerrillas did serious damage to Union lines of communication. General Grant ordered that if any of Mosby's men were captured, they were to be shot. Custer managed to capture and execute six of them. Two were shot, three were hanged, and one—a seventeen-year-old boy—was dragged through the street by two horses and shot in front of his mother, who begged Custer to desist. It wasn't a mother's tears that finally stopped the brutality, but rather Mosby's retaliation on any Union men he captured.

The Boy General was present at Appomattox. His commander, Philip Sheridan, purchased the pine table Grant used as a desk during Lee's surrender and gave it as a gift to Libbie Custer. She kept it, cherished it, and later passed it on to the Smithsonian, where it is still held.

In 1866, President Andrew Johnson toured the country with his cabinet and a handful of military heroes, including Grant and Custer. Was the golden boy beginning to dream political dreams? In all likelihood, yes.

But the war hero had some unpleasant postwar days. In 1867, he was court-martialed. No matter. General Sheridan needed him and had him reinstated the following year. Custer went on to achieve renown as an Indian fighter. He also wrote articles for *Turf, Field, and Farm*, the 1870s version of *Field and Stream*. His pen name was "Nomad."

He left Fort Abraham Lincoln on May 17, 1876. On June 25, with much of the country caught up in the centennial celebration, Custer and 270 troopers of the United States Cavalry were massacred at Little Bighorn by the Sioux, led by Sitting Bull. The Sioux not only killed Custer but rammed an arrow into his private parts. The only survivor of the battle was a horse named (ironically) Comanche. Custer the glorious was buried with honors at West Point.

His widow, his beloved Libbie, lived until 1933 and described their life together in *Boots and Saddles* and other books. In the 1940 movie *Santa Fe Trail*, Custer was portrayed by an actor named Ronald Reagan.

Jefferson Davis, Confederate President
(1808-1889)

SOUTHERN SPHINX

THE CONFEDERACY'S ONE AND ONLY president had an odd middle name—Finis, the Latin word for "last." He was the last of his family's large brood of children. Some say he was the last Southern gentleman as well.

Davis was a Kentucky boy, just like Abraham Lincoln. In fact, he was born less than a hundred miles from the cabin where Lincoln was born eight months later. Like Lincoln, he made his fame in another state. In Davis's case, that state was Mississippi, the home of his second wife, the devoted Varina. (His first wife, who died three months after their marriage, was the daughter of General—later President—Zachary Taylor.)

Except for his West Point education and a stint in the Mexican War (which brought him glory), Davis was never anything but a planter-politician, a role he loved. He served as a congressman, then as a senator, then as secretary of war under President Franklin Pierce, a bosom friend. Davis was genuinely good in his cabinet post, certainly a more energetic figure than the vacuous Pierce. One legacy to the United States Army (and later the Confederate army) from his days as secretary of war was the ankle-high "Jeff Davis boot." And he arranged to extend the West Point education from four years to five—a move everyone except the cadets themselves liked. He also formed a short-lived (but very sensible) camel corps in the Southwest.

Davis then returned to the Senate and became an outspoken champion of Southern rights. With the election of the hated Abraham Lincoln in 1860, Mississippi seceded from the Union, and Davis made his valediction speech in the Senate. With his military background, he expected a post in the Confederate army. He got more than he bargained for. While pruning roses at his plantation, Brierfield, he was informed he was the Confederacy's president. As gung-ho secessionist William L. Yancey put it, "The man and the hour have met."

When Davis took office in the State Capitol in Montgomery, Alabama, onlookers saw a stately man in his early fifties, extremely thin ("imperially slim," they said in those days), with a sometimes noticeable facial tic and a recurring problem with paralysis on one side of his face. In the days before TV, people didn't expect warm and cuddly politicians. They wanted their statesmen reserved and unshakable. Davis was that. Some thought him downright chilly. Others called him "the Sphinx," never knowing how to read him.

He had a thankless job ahead. The problem: how to be the chief executive of a nation formed from states that hated central authority. In his four years of enduring the presidency (his term was officially six years, but the Confederacy didn't last that long), Davis suffered enough abuse to last a lifetime. The Northern press, of course, despised him—he was a traitor, a rogue, a rat. Sadly, the Southern press often called him incompetent and a tyrant. Whatever went wrong in the Confederate States of America, Davis was the scapegoat.

He did have his flaws. He lacked the ability to delegate tasks, and he pretty much served as his own secretary of war (even though several other men officially held that demanding post). He was notorious for lec-

JEFFERSON
DAVIS

1808–1889

turing his generals on military matters, and he had a bad habit of protecting his "pets" (like the fractious Braxton Bragg) from being sacked. (For the record, he sometimes recognized true talent—like General Robert E. Lee.) Davis had been a fine United States senator, but he was entirely too unbending to be a good president, as even his wife admitted.

He found himself in a no-win situation. The South simply couldn't compete in military power and natural resources with the Union. Stubborn as Jeff was, Old Abe (who always referred to Davis as "that t'other feller") was stubborner, and Lincoln had the firepower to pursue the war to its bitter conclusion.

Davis suffered personal tragedy during the war. His little son Joe fell from a balcony at the Confederate White House and died. (Davis's two executive mansions—the first in Montgomery, the second in Richmond—were both called the Confederate White House, even though neither of them was ever white.) On July 4, 1864, Federals hosted a picnic at Davis's plantation for his liberated slaves. They also carted away everything in the home. Newspaper editors heaped abuse on Davis and Varina. No world leader ever recognized him as the legitimate president of a legitimate nation—except for Pope Pius IX, who, in a letter, referred to Davis as "President of the Confederacy."

By 1865, the Confederacy was ready to admit defeat, but Davis maintained his never-say-die attitude. Richmond fell to the Yanks in April, and Davis and his cabinet fled, carrying what remained of the Confederate treasury. With the Union armies nipping at their heels, he and his secretaries became a "government on wheels," heading into North Carolina, then Georgia. Union cavalry captured him on May 10. Never a whiner, Davis sat by his campfire and said with no emotion, "God's will be done." The Northern press painted the capture quite differently. Davis, they said, tried to escape capture by putting on his wife's cloak and hat. Northern political cartoonists had a field day showing the tall, lanky Davis (with his famous goatee) running while in drag.

At Fort Monroe in Hampton, Virginia, you can still see the gloomy cell where the ex-president was kept like an animal for two years. Davis's legs weren't shackled until he threw a plate of food in a guard's face. His keepers had been told not to shackle him unless provoked, and the plate of food did it. He resisted heartily, and it took four men to put the manacles on him. He slumped on his cot and wept like a baby.

The Federals intended to try him for treason, but as time passed, passion against the defeated South cooled. Newspaper editor Horace Greeley helped tremendously with an editorial protesting the treatment of Davis. Davis was released and never came to trial. (Considering that President Andrew Johnson had despised him since their days in Congress, it's a wonder Davis ever got out of prison.)

Those pieces of iron around his ankles were in fact a godsend, making both North and South see him as a martyr. He spent his last years traveling and writing his huge book, *The Rise and Fall of the Confederate Government*, which told more about the attitudes of Jefferson Davis than it did about the Confederacy itself.

Davis was hardly a well-loved character in his lifetime, but he has fared well as far as monuments go. Along with Generals Robert E. Lee and Stonewall Jackson, he is immortalized in the huge granite carving on Georgia's Stone Mountain. One other distinction: at his birthplace in Fairview, Kentucky, sits the largest memorial to any Confederate, the 350-foot Jefferson Davis Monument. Like many other Rebels, he fared better in memory than in real life.

Varina Davis, Confederate First Lady
(1826–1905)

SWEET WINNIE, JEFF'S HELPMEET

IF YOU WERE A WIDOWER and you remarried, would you take your second wife to visit your first wife's grave—on your honeymoon? Jefferson Davis did, but in the 1800s, that wasn't considered bad taste. Quite the opposite, in fact. It was a signal to the new wife that she had herself a sweet and sentimental man.

When Varina Howell of Natchez, Mississippi, met thirty-five-year-old Jefferson Davis, she was seventeen—a tall, statuesque brunette, not beautiful but serene looking, with striking eyes. She was dark in complexion, which in those days of idealized, ivory-skinned gentlewomen was a minus, not a plus. (Years later, Davis sacked one of his subordinates for referring to Varina as "an old squaw," a reference to her dark skin.) Varina was religious but also witty and well educated, having been tutored in the Greek and Latin classics.

Davis was a wealthy widower. His first wife (Sarah Knox Taylor, his beloved "Knoxie") was the daughter of Zachary Taylor. Varina found Davis a bit arrogant and chilly, but also handsome and polished. She also thought (as did many people) that he had the loveliest voice she had ever heard. Davis appreciated an intelligent woman who enjoyed discussing politics, even though he and Varina were of different parties (she was a Whig, he a Democrat). Her home was known as The Briers, and his was a plantation called Brierfield. Early in their marriage, his doting but domineering older brother, Joseph, devised a will that would keep Varina from inheriting any Davis property. Varina protested but finally gave in (the pattern for their whole marriage).

When Davis went to Congress, the woman he called "Sweet Winnie" became a model political wife, a gracious hostess, and a vivacious conversationalist on the subject of politics. (Considering she was only nineteen when he became a congressman, she was a remarkably fast learner.) She enjoyed her new life but disliked the stuffiness of the East Coast elitists. As she told Jefferson, "They take themselves so seriously that it is positively comical." Over the years, her unwillingness to play along with phonies made her a few enemies.

Before the war, she opposed secession and believed (correctly) that a separate Southern nation could never survive on its own. When the Confederacy was formed, she wrote, "We felt blood in the air." It was while she and her husband were pruning roses at Brierfield that they learned he had been elected the Confederacy's first (and only) president. Varina thus became the Confederacy's only first lady. She spent what she later called the worst years of her life in Richmond, the capital.

Varina understood her ambitious husband (whom she nicknamed "Banny"). She knew that though he had been a superb Mexican War officer and United States senator, he was not equipped to lead a nation. She wrote later, "He did not know the arts of the politician and would not practice them if understood, and he did know those of war." She understood that he was too rigid and way too sensitive to criticism to make it as a chief executive. (Lincoln, by contrast, was truly amazing in his ability to shrug off criticism.) Davis himself felt that he would have fared better as a general than as president. But the South had called him.

VARINA
DAVIS

1826–1905

Despite her charm and intelligence, some people thought Varina was meddlesome in politics. She probably wasn't, since no one, not even his wife, could boss Jefferson Davis around. She had a hopeless and thankless task: being the first lady in the capital of a country racked by war and deprivation. And she was prone to making the occasional faux pas that everyone would mumble about, like appearing at a public reception while she was visibly pregnant, which was simply not done in the 1860s. (A woman was supposed to be "confined" while pregnant.) Or like giving a man a deserved tongue-lashing on a Richmond street for abusing a horse. After that incident, the rumor went out that the president's wife was hot tempered.

Marriage to Jefferson Davis was no picnic. He was a good and faithful husband and father, but bossy as all get-out. He relied on his wife for many things. She became an expert at forging her husband's signature on official documents. She did this only when Davis was overworked or ill, and with his permission, of course. Handwriting experts aren't always sure just which signatures are really his. On the dark side, Varina had to bear the constant griping of newspaper editors, governors, Confederate congressmen, and the Southern populace at large, who made Jefferson Davis the scapegoat for everything bad.

But there was more to life than politics. She and Jefferson had six children, one of them born during the war. That child was the "Daughter of the Confederacy," Anne Varina Jefferson Davis, the younger "Winnie" who began life as "Piecake." One son, Joseph Evan, died in 1864 from a broken neck after a fall from a balcony of the Confederate White House (which was actually *gray*, for obvious reasons). Varina and Jefferson outlived all four of their sons.

Varina had some close friends, notably the famous diary keeper Mary Chesnut, whose still-popular journal tells much about both of the Davises. All of Varina's Richmond friends were, of course, political wives, and most of them, like Varina herself, were both gloomy and relieved when the South finally surrendered.

With the collapse of the Confederacy, her husband was a man on the run. He was put in prison—and literally chained down—in Fort Monroe, Virginia, while Varina herself (who was with him when he was captured) had to remain in Georgia, closely watched by the Federals. Husband and wife were not allowed to communicate in any way. The children were sent to Canada under the care of Varina's mother. Varina did what she could to secure her husband's release, which finally came in 1867. But the Davises never again lived as well as they had before the war. A friend generously arranged for them to live at Beauvoir, an estate near Biloxi, Mississippi. There, Jefferson, Varina, and young Winnie entertained various notables, making Beauvoir the "Post-Confederate White House." After Jefferson's death in 1889, Varina sold Beauvoir to the Sons of Confederate Veterans. For many years, it served as a Confederate veterans' home.

Varina then moved to Manhattan and supported herself by writing newspaper and magazine articles, many of them about (surprise!) the Civil War. Her one lengthy publication was *Jefferson Davis, Ex-President of the Confederate States of America: A Memoir by His Wife*. To the end, she maintained her prewar position: the South should not have seceded. The first lady was wiser than the secessionist "fire-eaters" who birthed the Confederacy and the grisly war that followed. Her writings showed that some ex-Confederates desired healing, not hate. After Grant's death, she published an article called "The Humanity of Grant." Her writings were illustrations of one of her mottoes, "Life is too short to bear animosities."

About her name: Her family pronounced it VA-REE-NUH, though almost everyone else said VA-RI-NUH. The unusual name was passed on to a daughter, granddaughter, and great-granddaughter. Mary Chesnut described the original Varina as "so clever, so brilliant, so warmhearted and considerate toward all who are around her," so it is well that the name lived on after her.

Jubal Early, Confederate General
(1816–1894)

UNRECONSTRUCTED CRANK

LONG BEFORE JERRY FALWELL, the most famous resident of Lynchburg, Virginia, was Old Jube. Until his death in 1894, Jube was a keeper of the flame for the Confederacy, a patriarch of the Lost Cause who assured Southerners (and any Northerners who dared to inquire) that the South had been right to secede, and that the saintly and dignified Robert E. Lee could have led the South to victory had he not been outnumbered by hordes of greedy Yankees. Cantankerous Old Jube gave public lectures and wrote magazine articles on the subject. Funny, considering that in 1861 he voted to keep his home state *in* the Union.

The man Lee fondly called "my bad old

man" was his opposite in almost every way. Old Jube rolled cigars in his mouth, drank more than was fitting, and cussed mightily. Yet he pleased Lee, for he fought like a demon under Stonewall Jackson (who frowned on Jube's swearing but respected his fighting moxie). Some called him "Jubal E.," a play on the religious meaning of the word *jubilee*. (Like his parents, Joab and Ruth, Jubal had a biblical name, if not a biblical mouth. Early was one of the few people who could swear in front of the saintly Lee.)

General Moxley Sorrel wrote that Early's "irritable disposition and biting tongue made him anything but popular." But like everyone else, Sorrel praised the general's abilities. Early didn't give two hoots about the impression he made on others. Julia, his mistress for two decades, bore him four children (one of whom was named Jubal), but Old Jube never married. He and Julia had a falling-out in 1871, and she wed another man.

Jube had the look of a true character. He had the dark, piercing eyes and the gray beard (but not the sanctity) of an Old Testament prophet. He wore a slouch hat topped with a black ostrich plume. He stood six feet but appeared shorter (and older) because of his rheumatism. His high-pitched, nasal voice sounded, some said, like an old woman's.

Steady streams of tobacco juice and profanity spewed from his lips. He carried a canteen that (so his enemies said) contained whiskey.

Early, a lawyer, was a delegate to the Virginia secession convention in 1861. At that time, he was a staunch Unionist, maybe because his home turf was tobacco country, which needed its Northern markets. Even after the firing on Fort Sumter, Early voted to remain in the Union. He called the United States "the fairest fabric of government that was ever erected." Even so, as a West Point alumnus, he offered his military services to his state. He wrote later that any doubts he had were dispelled by "the frenzied clamor of the people of the North for war upon their former brethren of the South."

The former Union man scored some points at the Confederacy's first grand victory. Early commanded the brigade that turned the tide at First Manassas. For this, he was made a brigadier general. Lee and Jackson praised him highly for his performance in several Virginia battles.

But it was the scare he caused in Washington that made Old Jube's reputation. Promoted to lieutenant general in May 1864, Early was given a major task: threaten Baltimore and Washington, the aim being to divert Grant's troops from Richmond. (It was a

JUBAL
EARLY

1816–1894

game called "Whose Capital Is in Greater Jeopardy?") With his small but spunky Army of the Valley, which never boasted more than fourteen thousand men, Early raided Maryland and collected $220,000 in tribute from the towns of Frederick and Hagerstown. Then, on July 11, his troops threatened to enter D.C.

In the almost-raid on Washington, some of Jube's sharpshooters took aim at a tall figure in a high hat on the parapet of Fort Stevens—but they missed Lincoln. One man was shot dead three feet from the president. Early told one officer, "We haven't taken Washington, but we've scared Abe Lincoln like hell!" Yet many Southern papers condemned Early for his failure to take the capital.

The unintended result of Early's raid on Washington was to bring hellacious retribution on the South, the Shenandoah Valley of Virginia in particular. Grant ordered Phil Sheridan to sack the fertile valley for food supplies. Early was criticized for losing the valley to the Federals, but it is doubtful that anyone else could have prevented it.

Old Jube was incensed at the destruction of property in the Shenandoah. He got vengeance on July 30 and 31, 1864. Under his orders, the town of Chambersburg, Pennsylvania, was told to fork over $100,000 in gold or $300,000 in greenbacks as recompense for

Union destruction of Virginia property, else the town would be "laid in ashes in retaliation." Because some Rebel soldiers had already begun plundering, the citizens refused to pay. The Confederates torched a warehouse, the courthouse, the town hall, and much of the rest of the town. Damages amounted to about $1.5 million. Early considered it just.

When the war ended, Early had no intention of living in a reconstructed South. Fearing Federal vengeance for what he'd done to Chambersburg, he fled to Mexico but wound up in Canada, where he wrote his self-serving memoirs, published in 1867. After Andrew Johnson's pardon of former Confederates in 1869, Jube returned to Virginia and practiced law. More to his liking was a later job as commissioner of the Louisiana State Lottery, a post that gave him leisure to lecture and write articles on the war. Playing the role of an unreconstructed Rebel to the hilt, the old soldier wore only gray and made no apologies for his actions during the war, especially the burning of Chambersburg. He was an officer in both the Southern Historical Society and the Association of the Army of Northern Virginia. In his view, the agrarian South never truly lost, but only succumbed to the overwhelming numbers of men from the industrial North.

Jube also worked to defend the most

controversial part of his record: Gettysburg. That Confederate defeat in early July 1863 unleashed a flood of books and articles. Why did the South lose? Some blamed Early. His actions there were controversial. His hesitation on July 1, when Cemetery and Culp's Hills were still vulnerable, was a major blunder. In his postwar rewriting of Confederate history, Early largely succeeded (in his lifetime, anyway) in smearing General James Longstreet's actions at Gettysburg. Longstreet, reconstructed to the point of—horrors!—being a Republican and a friend of Grant, was Early's bogeyman. Lee, on the other hand, was his angel. Probably no one helped forge the image of the divine Lee more than the foulmouthed Old Jube. The man with no religion thus helped create one: the Lost Cause.

Richard S. Ewell, Confederate General
(1817–1872)

BALD AND LISPING REBEL BIRD

EWELL AND ANOTHER Rebel general, Jubal Early, were apparently vying for the title of M.P.—Master of Profanity. Ewell and Early were both characters, the sort of people who make history more entertaining reading than fiction.

In looks, Ewell was even more of a character than Early. The bearded, five-foot-seven general was a walking cartoon: hooked nose, bulging eyes, high-pitched voice, volcanic temper. He lisped, which must have added humor to his cuss words. His bald head (called "bomb-shaped" by a fellow general) was often cocked to one side, birdlike. He was variously known as "Old Baldy," "Old Baldhead," and "Bald

Dick." Like Stonewall Jackson, under whose command he constantly groused (and won battles), Ewell suffered, or thought he suffered, dyspepsia. In the days before acid blockers, this was taken with great seriousness. The one food that did not upset his gastric tract was frumenty, a bland, wheat-and-water preparation served with honey and raisins—the 1860s version of Cream of Wheat. As with most hypochondriacs, his ailments were the chief subject of his conversation.

And then there was the wooden leg. Old Baldy led a regiment out to a Federal line at Groveton, Virginia, in 1862. Stupidly, some of his men shouted, "Here's General Ewell, boys!" This effectively served as a signal for the Yanks to begin firing. Ewell's left knee was shattered, requiring amputation of the leg. He was subsequently fitted with a wooden one. Later, at Gettysburg, the wooden leg was hit by a bullet. To another general, he cackled, "It don't hurt a bit to be shot in a wooden leg."

While recuperating in Richmond after the amputation, Old Baldy was nursed by someone warm and familiar: Lizinka Campbell Brown, the Tennessee sweetheart he had lost to another man in his younger days. She was now a wealthy widow. They married in May 1863, just after Stonewall Jackson's death at Chancellorsville, a death that led to Ewell's

assumption of Jackson's old post as head of the Second Corps in Lee's army. Ewell and "Mrs. Brown" (he sometimes introduced her as "my wife, Mrs. Brown") had a brief honeymoon before the general led his corps north into Pennsylvania. He was preparing to attack Harrisburg, Pennsylvania's capital, when Lee summoned him to Gettysburg.

Like practically every Confederate leader who fought there, Ewell was blamed for the loss at Gettysburg. Specifically, he was faulted for failing to capture Cemetery Hill. Though historians continue to refight the battle, it is doubtful that Old Baldy would have cared. He was quite unlike most Civil War generals in that he gave nary a thought to fame or creating a personal legend. The peculiar little lisping man was deeply devoted to the Confederacy, not to his own ego. He said that it took "a dozen blunders to lose Gettysburg" and admitted he had committed "a good many of them."

The birdlike Ewell was indeed a rare bird. His men adored him, quirks and all. He fought with brio, but he had to be given precise directions. He had no imagination, no ability to see beyond the obvious—which was why the enigmatic Jackson nettled him so.

Jackson and Ewell respected each other's soldiering ability, but Jackson's habit of never

RICHARD S.
EWELL

1817–1872

explaining his plans to subordinates drove the high-strung Ewell to distraction. He constantly griped that he was serving under a man "mad as a March hare." The foul-mouthed Ewell once observed the devout Jackson at a worship service. As often happened, Jackson dozed off during the sermon. Old Baldy asked in exasperation, "What is the use of General Jackson going to church? He sleeps all the time!" Ewell referred to Jackson (though not to his face, of course) as an "old fool," even though Ewell was the older of the two. A perplexed and fretting Ewell did receive comfort from Jackson's religion on one occasion. He rode to see Stonewall and arrived just in time to hear Jackson's chaplain, Reverend Dabney, preach on the Bible verse, "Come unto me, all ye that labor and are heavy-laden, and I will give you rest." It soothed Ewell's fretful mind momentarily.

After his marriage, Old Baldy cleaned up his vocabulary under Lizinka's influence and became a churchgoer (lisping God's name in prayer instead of in vain) and a kinder, gentler gentleman. Some sniped that Lizinka dominated her husband, not only managing his domestic life but meddling in military matters as well. But she also aided her husband when things got rough. At war's end, Ewell was captured and sent to Fort Warren military prison in Boston. Lizinka had known President Andrew Johnson when he was governor of Tennessee, and she went to him to plead for her husband's release. Johnson was rude to her, making some tasteless joke about her having married a one-legged man. She then went to see Ulysses S. Grant, who said he would be pleased to aid "my old friend Ewell." Grant then ordered Ewell's release.

Old Baldy and Lizinka settled on her plantation at Spring Hill, Tennessee. During the winter of 1872, he fell ill with pneumonia. Nursing him back to health, she contracted the disease herself and died. Her husband followed her forty-eight hours later.

Before he died, Old Baldy insisted that there be "nothing reflecting against the government of the United States" on his tombstone.

David Glasgow Farragut, Union Admiral
(1801–1870)

GULF GO-GETTER

"DAMN THE TORPEDOES! Full speed ahead!" is one of the great quotes from the Civil War (or any war). It came from the lips of one of America's great sea dogs. Before he issued that profane order, Farragut—lashed to the mast of his flagship—had prayed, "O God, who created man and gave him reason, direct me what to do. Shall I go on?" He did.

He had been going a long time. Note Farragut's birth year: 1801. Many Civil War biggies were veterans of the Mexican War. Farragut went back much farther—to the War of 1812, when young David, age eleven, was a midshipman in the United States Navy.

Farragut's father was born on the Mediterranean island of Minorca. James Glasgow

Farragut (he wasn't *David* yet) was born at Campbell's Station, Tennessee, near Knoxville (which is nowhere near any sea).

It was when the boy began serving under navy man David Porter, Jr., that he changed his name from James to David, in honor of his mentor. When Porter caught young David with tobacco juice seeping from his lips, he clapped his hands over the boy's mouth until he was forced to swallow the wad. This had the desired effect: David never again used tobacco in any form.

When the Civil War began, Farragut was living in the great naval town of Norfolk, Virginia. But unlike true-blue Virginians, he never agonized over the choice between Virginia and the United States. He was strictly a Union man, and he moved his family to New York. Like many Southerners in the Union forces, he had to endure the skepticism of Northerners who doubted his loyalty.

New Orleans, queen city of the Gulf and the grand metropolis of the Confederacy, was Farragut's first great conquest. Working with General Benjamin Butler (known as "Beast" when he later governed the embittered city), Farragut led an amphibious assault on New Orleans in April 1862. The angry citizens greeted him by setting the waterfront on fire, which forced him to anchor his fleet far from

the flames. Ten thousand Confederates fled New Orleans, torching fifteen thousand bales of cotton, a dozen large ships, and several steamboats. Farragut was incensed that William Mumford, a professional gambler, removed the Union flag from the United States Mint. He threatened to bombard the place unless the flag was respected. One New Orleans woman emptied her slop jar on Farragut as he passed beneath her balcony. He was lucky in that, unlike Butler (who stayed and was despised), he left New Orleans soon after its capture.

When he arrived in Washington, Farragut was a national hero. One observer called the sixty-one-year-old sea dog "a most jolly, conversable, genial old boy; clear-headed, well-informed, and perhaps a little dogmatic, but not much." Newspapermen christened him "Daring Dave" and "the American Viking."

He was less successful in his next venture. In the spring and summer of 1862, Farragut attempted to subdue Vicksburg, Mississippi. The military governor of the city responded to Farragut's call to surrender in this way: "Mississippians don't know, and refuse to learn, how to surrender. If Commodore Farragut can teach them, let him come and try." He couldn't.

Another Gulf port, Mobile, was Farragut's second great achievement. Since the fall of

DAVID
GLASGOW
FARRAGUT

1801–1870

New Orleans, the Alabama city had been a key port for the Confederacy. The Rebels knew the importance of the site and fortified it accordingly. This included planting sea mines—known as "torpedoes" in those days—throughout Mobile Bay. When Farragut's fleet arrived in August 1864, one of his ships, the *Tecumseh*, struck a torpedo and sank. The Union ships behind halted while the Confederate guns at Fort Morgan blasted away at them. On board the *Hartford*, the determined Farragut, having no intention of pausing under Fort Morgan's guns, issued his famous order. The torpedoes must have been damned adequately, for none exploded.

Confederate admiral Franklin Buchanan (known as "Old Buck") put up a stiff resistance, and the South's notorious ram *Tennessee* was in the thick of the fight. But the Yanks seriously damaged the ironclad, and Buchanan himself was injured. He was finally forced to surrender.

Farragut demanded that Fort Morgan surrender "to prevent the unnecessary sacrifice of human life." The fort's defender was an old Norfolk naval buddy, Richard L. Page, first cousin of Robert E. Lee (and an uncanny look-alike). Page responded, "I am prepared to sacrifice life, and will only surrender when I have no means of defense." But eventually, cut off from Confederate supplies, Page waved the

white flag. The battle closed the port of Mobile to the outside world.

The victory at Mobile resulted in Farragut's promotion to vice admiral. He thus became the first Union naval officer to hold that title. (Prior to his promotion, commodore was the top rank in the navy.) After the war, he was made full admiral, again becoming the first man in the United States Navy to hold that title. (Note: The Confederacy beat the Union to the punch, making Franklin Buchanan a full admiral in 1862.)

Did Farragut have Russians in his fleet? During the war, negotiations with Russia for the purchase of Alaska ground to a halt. But the Russians were still interested. As a goodwill gesture, they "loaned" Farragut five hundred men for his assault on Mobile Bay. Whether they were among his men during the actual attack has been debated.

The great Horace Greeley, newspaper editor and man of many opinions, strongly urged Republicans to nominate anyone besides Lincoln in 1864. He suggested Grant, Sherman, and Beast Butler as presidential candidates, with Farragut as running mate. Like many of Greeley's crackpot but well-intentioned fancies (including his own presidential run in 1872), it came to nothing.

Farragut was still spry at age sixty. He had

a habit of turning a handspring on his birth-
day just to prove he was still in shape.

He died in 1870. Conspicuously absent
from the admiral's funeral was President
Ulysses S. Grant, who apparently held a
grudge against Farragut for not supporting him
in the 1868 election. For this, Grant was in-
undated with scores of nasty letters wondering how one Union hero could snub another.

Nathan Bedford Forrest, Confederate General
(1821–1877)

TENNESSEE CENTAUR

"War means fightin' and fightin' means killin'." "Forward, men, and mix with 'em." "The way to whip an enemy is to git 'em skeered, and then keep the skeer on 'em." "Shoot at everything blue and keep up the skeer." A backwoods farmer with almost no education, Forrest was one of the most quoted and quotable men of the Civil War.

"General," a woman once asked him, "why is it the hair on your head is gray and your beard is black?" Straight-faced, he replied, "Ma'am, it's because I work my head more'n I work my jaws."

Forrest's middle name was derived from his rural birthplace, Bedford County, Tennessee. He personified the ornery, hardworking dirt farmers who far outnumbered the highfalutin' plantation masters like Robert E. Lee and Jefferson Davis.

His father died when Nathan was sixteen, and Forrest became chief provider for a large brood. He may have missed his dad as breadwinner, but he probably didn't miss the frequent and brutal beatings the old man had given him. Nathan proceeded to make a small fortune in a lucrative business in those days— buying and selling slaves.

When war broke out, Forrest enlisted as a private. Despite having no military training whatsoever, he rose to the rank of lieutenant general in three years. The Confederate army was packed with West Point graduates ("P'inters," Forrest called them, mostly in disgust). Forrest, on the other hand, made his military reputation with sheer gutsiness. He also knew something about killing, claiming at war's end that he had personally killed more men than any other American general. (This included one of his own subordinates, whom he killed in a brawl.) His horses knew something about killing too—or, more accurately, something about being killed. The "Wizard of the Saddle," as Forrest was known, claimed he had twenty-nine horses shot from under him. The men he called his "Critter Company" idolized the valorous man with martial fire in his blood.

Forrest once told his soldiers, "Men, if you will do as I say I will always lead you to victory." Indeed, he did not like to lose. When three Confederate generals agreed to surrender Fort Donelson to U. S. Grant, Forrest stamped off in disgust, saying, "I did not come here to surrender my command!" He led his cavalrymen away, braving a blinding winter storm and an ice-swollen river. Better chilly noses than surrendering to the Bluecoats.

"That devil Forrest," as he was dubbed by his Yankee opponents, galloped to fame in the western regions of the Confederacy, far from the better-known battlefields of Virginia. But his doings did not go unnoticed. William T. Sherman once sent a message to Secretary of War Stanton that read, "There will never be peace in Tennessee until Forrest is dead." (After the war, Sherman referred to Forrest as "the most remarkable man our Civil War produced.") In one noted cavalry battle, Forrest prevailed with thirty-five hundred men against the Union's eight thousand. Having gone on record as saying, "Get there firstest with the mostest," he proved that having the mostest wasn't always necessary. (Probably without knowing it, the country boy had stated in brief the battle philosophy of the man who most intrigued American officers: Napoleon.)

In 1864, Forrest's forces captured three Union boats, which were then used in a raid

NATHAN
BEDFORD
FORREST

1821–1877

on a Union depot in Tennessee. The brassy Forrest thus claimed he had set up his own Confederate navy.

He was one of many Rebel generals who detested the obstreperous commander of the Army of Tennessee, Braxton Bragg. After the Confederate victory at Chickamauga, Forrest begged Bragg to pursue the Yanks, but Bragg would not. Tired of Bragg, Forrest demanded, and got, his own independent command in Mississippi.

The most notorious action in Forrest's career was the 1864 massacre at Fort Pillow. That Mississippi River fort in Tennessee was held by 295 white and 262 black Federals. Forrest took the fort, killing 231 men in the process. According to Union accounts, the killings took place *after* the fort had surrendered. Following the war, a woman confronted him, asking if he really was the man responsible for the Fort Pillow massacre. Forrest rose up bristling and said, "Yes, ma'am, I killed the men and women for my soldiers' dinner and ate the babies myself for breakfast." The woman ran out of the room screaming.

His name still inspires controversy. A city park named for him in Memphis provoked protests, some antagonists claiming that a racist general's name had no business being attached to public land.

Under his wife's influence, Forrest made his peace with God in his later years, perhaps hoping that God would forgive him for being "that devil Forrest."

William Lloyd Garrison, Abolitionist
(1805–1879)

CAIN-RAISING RADICAL

ABRAHAM LINCOLN got all the raves because it was he who issued the Emancipation Proclamation. But with all due respect to Lincoln, the toilers in the vineyard of abolition had done much of the spadework for the cause thirty years before the Civil War. Of course, those abolitionists were much less likable than the folksy, log-cabin Lincoln. They were nearly as unpopular in the North as in the South. They were that painful phenomenon we sometimes meet: people who are *morally right* but downright *irritating*. Perhaps they irritate because the line between *righteous* and *holier than thou* is so thin.

One of the abolitionist luminaries was

Garrison, whose portrait tells much: he was intense, humorless, probably no fun at all at a party. In 1831, he founded his famous Boston newspaper, *The Liberator*, in which he declared, "On this subject [abolition] I do not wish to think, or speak, or write, with moderation. . . . I will be harsh as truth and as uncompromising as justice. . . . I am in earnest—I will not equivocate—I will not excuse—I will not retreat a single inch. *And I will be heard.*" He sounded about as subtle as an Old Testament prophet—and America has never been comfortable with such people. Granted, a revival preacher calling individuals to repent of their sins was (and still is) part of the American scene. But Garrison and his fellow abolitionists condemned a whole section of the nation—the South. America's "original sin" was slavery.

The gospel of abolition was centered in Massachusetts, Garrison's birthplace. The old Puritan fire there had never died out, just burned in a different form. The Puritans of the 1600s emphasized individuals' sins and redemption and divided the world into the righteous and the damned. The neo-Puritans of the 1800s divided the world into the abolitionists and the damned. The abolitionists foresaw a violent, horrible end—a revolt of slaves, perhaps, or even a civil war. Small won-

der that most Southerners came to despise Massachusetts above all other Northern states. During the war, Union general George McClellan said that he detested Massachusetts (the abolitionist hub) and South Carolina (the secessionist hub) and would "rejoice to see both states extinguished. Both were and always had been ultra-mischievous." More than a few historians have suggested that without the extremists in those two states, there might never have been a war.

Back to 1831. It happened that the year Garrison launched his paper was also the year of Nat Turner's bloody slave rebellion in Virginia, which resulted in the death of several whites. Thus, two messages were driven home to Southerners, particularly slave owners: slaves could be provoked to kill their masters, and when they did, those meddlesome abolitionists would applaud it.

Garrison, who had been a deeply religious boy, became an abolitionist under Quaker influence. The Quakers were almost the only Christian denomination that prohibited members from owning slaves (even though some did anyway).

The Liberator never actually sold all that widely, but Garrison's reputation and influence were far wider than the paper's circulation. He courted persecution and often received it. He

once stood for an hour with a rope around his neck, fearing that the mob around him fully intended to put it to use. When some hooligans were dragging Garrison through the streets of Boston, the sight so impressed Wendell Phillips that he jumped on the abolition bandwagon (and later became almost as famous as Garrison).

Slave owners and the politicians who kowtowed to them were Garrison's favorite targets. Though many in the South worked to keep *The Liberator* from circulating there, Southern newspapers loved to quote Garrison's antislavery harangues, holding them up as examples of Yankee extremism. The abolitionists who called themselves Christians (probably a majority) claimed they would do away with slavery not through violence but through "the power of love" and "moral suasion." Yet there was little evidence of "love power" in Garrison's anti-South tirades.

At a Fourth of July rally in 1854, Garrison burned a copy of the United States Constitution, proclaiming, "So perish all compromises with tyranny." In his eyes, the Constitution (which he called a "covenant with death and hell") was a mockery of freedom and equality, since it did not prohibit slavery. Garrison called for the North to secede from the United States and free itself from the corruption of slavery.

After the war began but before the Emancipation Proclamation, Lincoln got his share of abuse from Garrison. The righteous editor described him as "a man of very small calibre," one who "had better be at his old business of splitting rails than at the head of a government like ours." He also described Lincoln as "stumbling, halting, prevaricating, irresolute, weak, besotted." Lincoln's strategy of waiting until just the right moment to free the slaves drove the abolitionists bananas. (He was a politician who focused on the possible; they were radicals who focused on the ideal, with no place for compromise or hesitation.) When Lincoln finally issued the proclamation, Garrison did relent, referring to it as "a great historic event, sublime, momentous, and beneficent." He announced with deep satisfaction that Lincoln the "rail-splitter" had become Lincoln the "chain-breaker."

When the American flag was officially raised again over Fort Sumter in 1865, Garrison was there as a guest of honor.

A surprising thing happened in 1869: Garrison officially disbanded his group, the American Anti-Slavery Society. Once the Fifteenth Amendment was put forward to guarantee voting rights to blacks, the society's mission was completed. It was a rare case of a pressure group dissolving once its work was done. Garrison looked back on forty years of writing and speaking and being heckled, beaten, jailed, and cursed by Northerners and Southerners alike. He believed it had all been worth it, that he had finished the race.

Or at least he had finished *one* race. Radicals seldom retire. Having settled the race problem (or so he thought), Garrison spent his remaining years combating liquor, prostitution, and injustice against Indians. Slightly ahead of his time, he also advocated giving women the vote.

Were he alive now, he would no doubt be politically correct.

Ulysses S. Grant, Union General
(1822–1885)

A BAG OF MEAL, WITH GRIT

THE UNION'S GREAT war hero and a two-term United States president, Grant never made an impression with his looks. He was five-foot-eight and had a scraggly beard and a generally dumpy look. One observer said that he sat astride his horse "like a bag of meal." The South was pleased that *its* hero, the classy, dignified Robert E. Lee, looked like a leader. But Grant, lacking the look, definitely had the grit to lead.

No one predicted it. "Lyss" Grant from Ohio began life as Hiram Ulysses Grant. Thanks to a slip-up by the congressman who got him appointed to West Point, he went down on the school's roll—and throughout history—as Ulysses Simpson

Grant (Simpson was his mother's maiden name). He signed himself "U. H. Grant" during his cadet years.

Other than being a good horseman, Grant didn't make a splash at West Point. Upon his entry, he was only five-foot-one—just a hair above the minimum requirement. He preferred reading romance novels to manuals on tactics. In fact, he had not wanted to go to West Point at all, and had done so only to please his dad. While there, he hoped that Congress would close the academy so he could go home. (Unlikely as it sounds, there were people in Congress in those days who seriously wanted to shut down West Point.)

Hiram—or Ulysses—became "Captain Sam" to his pals. (His initials led to his being called "United States Grant," then "Uncle Sam Grant," and finally just "Sam.") He fought in the Mexican War (as did almost every Civil War hero), but his military career went downhill after that. The bourbon-loving Grant resigned in 1854 to avoid being court-martialed for his drinking. He didn't succeed outside the army either. Grant was a flop at farming; at one point, he was reduced to peddling firewood. He called his Missouri property "Hardscrabble Farm," a spoof on the pretentious names other planters gave their farms.

When the Civil War began, the Mexican War veteran got no encouragement to join the Union army. But he managed to whip an Illinois infantry unit into shape and made enough of an impression to be promoted to brigadier general.

His star rose quickly. He captured Forts Donelson and Henry in Tennessee and earned the famous nickname "Unconditional Surrender," which was what he had demanded from the forts. The capture of Donelson and Henry was a tremendous morale booster. Northern church bells rang, and Grant's unconditional-surrender ultimatum to General Buckner (an old friend) was widely quoted.

Grant was the man of the hour, but his glory dimmed a little after the Battle of Shiloh. He redeemed himself with the long and successful siege of Vicksburg, Mississippi, then earned a three-star rank and the title of general in chief after the successes around Chattanooga.

Lincoln adored Grant and summarized his abilities in this simple way: "He fights." After dealing with the vain, dawdling (and over-rated) George McClellan, Lincoln was pleased to find a military commander who preferred fighting over trumpeting his ego.

Grant's cross-eyed wife, Julia, was his prop in life, loving and comforting him when he was down. Whenever he was away from her for an extended period, he grew depressed and

ULYSSES S.
GRANT

1822–1885

boozy. The silent man was chilly and aloof toward almost everyone except his beloved wife and kids. He seemed to have no warm feelings toward other family members, his avaricious father in particular.

Like the South's Stonewall Jackson, Grant kept his own counsel. One observer said he kept a "padlock on his mouth." But like many quiet men, he had nervous energy. He smoked cigars and whittled constantly, reducing his sticks to splinters but never carving anything in particular. Grant was a pipe smoker before his victory at Fort Donelson, but afterward many admirers sent him cigars, which then became part of his standard attire.

He was a fighter, but not one who enjoyed killing. In fact, he preferred siege tactics (and was good at them) to outright battles. He couldn't stand to see blood on his plate and insisted that his meat be cooked *very* well done. Though some historians have called Grant a butcher, he has never had the villainous reputation of William T. Sherman. Grant's usual question after a Union victory was "How many prisoners?" He seemed concerned that the enemy be captured, not maimed or killed. Perhaps he had a compassionate streak. He definitely did *not* have a "take no prisoners" mentality.

Lyss and Julia were supposed to attend the play *Our American Cousin* with the Lincolns on the night of the assassination, but they changed their minds at the last minute. Grant subsequently showed real compassion by preventing the new president, Andrew Johnson, from bringing Lee to trial for treason.

After the war, Grant was *the* political success story—sort of. Like many veterans both North and South, he entered politics (as a Republican, naturally). His campaign slogan, of his own devising, was "Let us have peace." He reached the top rung by becoming a two-term president, but historians don't rate him highly. He was, at age forty-six, the youngest president elected until that time—and also the least experienced in politics. In his inaugural address, he admitted that "the office has come to me unsought; I commence its duties untrammeled." Grant was decent and respectable but a poor judge of men, and his political cronies were notoriously corrupt. Even so, Grant could have served a third term, but he declined.

Famous and admired as he was, Grant fell upon hard times in his later years, mostly because a business partner, Ferdinand Ward, proved an incredibly good swindler. The retired general and president found himself in desperate need of money. Mark Twain, a fervent admirer, convinced him to write his memoirs, and Grant proved a better writer than a president. He finished his highly readable memoirs (published by Mark Twain) just a few days before his death from throat cancer. His work is all the more remarkable when you consider that he was in excruciating pain while writing. His widow made a small fortune from the memoirs.

Grant had one oddity: he loathed music. He was apparently tone-deaf (like Stonewall Jackson, although Jackson liked music). Grant said he could distinguish only two tunes. "One was 'Yankee Doodle' and the other wasn't," he wrote. He would go out of his way to avoid hearing a band play. Considering all the music performed in his honor, he must have had some uncomfortable moments.

A direct descendant, U. S. Grant V, is still living.

Remember the old joke, "Who's buried in Grant's Tomb?" The majestic tomb is, by the way, in Riverside Park in New York.

Rose Greenhow, Confederate Spy and Diplomat
c. 1815–1864

KEEPER OF THE LITTLE BIRDS

ROSE O'NEAL GREENHOW'S life raises a question: Why hasn't Hollywood discovered her yet?

Her early years are a mystery. No one knows for sure precisely when and where Rose O'Neal was born. The only clues are her later boast that "I am a Southern woman, and I thank God that no drop of Yankee blood ever polluted my veins!" Most likely, she was born in a small Maryland farm community near Washington and was orphaned at an early age.

For certain, Rose arrived in Washington in 1827, when she was about twelve. She stayed with her aunt, who kept the Old Capitol Boarding House, a first-class hos-

telry that served as a makeshift capitol following the British burning of the real Capitol during the War of 1812. When Rose came to live
in the boardinghouse, it was still populated by
many congressmen, who made it their home
away from home. She grew up to become a
political junkie. She was especially dazzled by
the brilliant man from South Carolina, the
great John C. Calhoun, whom she later called
"the best and wisest man of this century." His
beliefs about states' rights and the right of secession were fixed in her mind.

The people at the boardinghouse called
her the "Wild Rose." To everyone's surprise,
the lovely, vivacious girl married Robert
Greenhow, a pleasant but fairly dull man who
worked as a translator for the State Department. His boss was Secretary of State James
Buchanan, and Rose came to know "Old Buck"
well before he became president.

Rose was a loyal wife and mother—and
also an upward climber who invited all the
right people to the Greenhow home to advance her husband's career and to satisfy her
own craving for politics. Usually gracious and
charming, she was open about her distaste for
abolitionists: "My blood boils when I think of
them!"

After her husband's death and soon after
secession, Colonel Thomas Jordan (still in Fed-

eral uniform but preparing to join the Rebels)
enlisted Rose in the Confederate cause. She
and Jordan arranged a special code for their
messages. She told him that she would send
information "by my little birds," referring to
girls and women, mostly of the lower classes,
whom she could send south. Jordan became a
trusted aide to General Beauregard.

Rose's "little birds" were busy in the summer of 1861. Somehow (she never divulged
exactly how), she got copies of the minutes
of every Union high command meeting and
then sent coded summaries to Colonel Jordan.
Whatever her sources, they were reliable. Before First Manassas, Beauregard was well informed of the Union's plans. She sent her
messages via a Maryland country girl, who,
looking like a bumpkin, drove her vegetable
wagon across the Potomac with no hassles
from Union sentries. Her messages convinced
Beauregard to telegraph Jefferson Davis in
Richmond to urgently request reinforcements.
The Rebel victory at Manassas was a great
morale builder for the South.

Rose's nemesis was Scotsman Allan
Pinkerton, a detective enlisted by Union general George McClellan as Washington's chief
spy catcher. Shortly after Manassas, Pinkerton
and his men began their surveillance of
Greenhow. On one occasion, the short, stocky

ROSE
GREENHOW

c. 1815–1864

Pinkerton stood on the shoulders of two of his agents and silently raised a parlor window so he could eavesdrop on a conversation between Rose and an army captain. The two were going over a map, and Pinkerton realized the captain was showing her the positions of fortified gun posts around Washington.

Going for a stroll the next morning, Rose was discreetly told by one of her "little birds" that Pinkerton had arrived at her house and was waiting to arrest her. Carrying herself like a queen, Rose allowed the detective into her home. She had some coded letters on her and wondered what she would do if (horrors!) Pinkerton wanted a body search. So she insisted (it being August) that she be allowed to change into a fresh dress, at which time she managed to get the messages out of her clothes and into a hiding place. It was well that she did, since Pinkerton brought in a woman detective to search her. A friend dropped by for a visit, and Rose got her to conceal the coded letters in her boots. The letters then departed the house with no problem.

In her diary, Rose wrote, "The devil is no match for a clever woman." Life—and spying—went on even under surveillance. She probably wheedled information out of Massachusetts senator Henry Wilson and (though we can't be certain) may have become his mistress. Her home was gradually turned into a prison for "secesh dames." Pinkerton ordered her room's shutters nailed shut so she couldn't wave to anyone outside. She then wrote a long, self-pitying letter of protest to Secretary of State Seward. Through her "birds," she also sent a copy of the letter to a Richmond newspaper. Its appearance there convinced Seward and others that she still enjoyed too much communication with the outside world. On the other hand, the outside world learned that people were being detained and that habeas corpus had been thrust aside. So Rose became (as she planned) a martyr to the Lincoln administration's wartime paranoia. As she wrote in her diary, "They dare not hang me, but they are afraid to release me."

Pinkerton's men eventually dismantled practically every piece of her furniture, but they found nothing. So they forced her out of her house and into (ironically) her childhood home, the Old Capitol Boarding House, now the Old Capitol Prison. Rose made one comical attempt to escape in a vegetable peddler's cart, cracking his whip and yelling, "I'm off for Dixie!" The prison guards caught her quickly.

Later, she and another "secesh dame" were swapped for two Pinkerton spies the

Confederacy had captured. In effect, she was deported to the Confederacy. Her destination was Richmond, where she was the toast of the town. Jefferson Davis told her, "But for you, there would have been no Battle of Manassas." In her diary, she wrote of the meeting as "the proudest moment of my whole life."

Yearning for adventure, she became a Confederate diplomat in Europe. In France, Emperor Napoleon III received her warmly. But despite her charm and pleading, he had no intention of recognizing the Confederacy as a nation. In London, she was received by Queen Victoria—but again, no official recognition for the Confederacy was forthcoming. She charmed the British upper classes, who generally sympathized with Southern aristocrats. While in England, she published her book, *My Imprisonment and the First Year of Abolition Rule at Washington*, in which she hoped to show the world how the Lincoln administration was abusing human rights and civil liberties. The book sold, but it was not the nation-shaking work she had hoped. Even so, she left England with a few prizes: an engagement to an English lord, several thousands dollars in gold (which the Confederacy desperately needed), and (as in every good spy story) a case full of mysterious papers.

For her voyage home on the *Condor*, she had gold pieces sewn into her clothing. Fastened to her neck by a chain was a huge leather bag holding more gold. Heading for the port at Wilmington, North Carolina, the *Condor* was pursued by a Federal blockading vessel and ran onto a sand bar. Rose insisted on being let down in a small boat and rowed to shore by two members of the *Condor's* crew. But the small boat capsized in the waves. The two men managed to swim to shore, but Rose drowned, weighed down by the gold.

Henry W. Halleck, Union General
(1815–1872)

DESK JOCKEY IN CHIEF

INTELLECTUALS USUALLY make poor soldiers, and Halleck's nickname, "Old Brains," pretty much sums up his ability as a commander. A man who preferred military matters to take place in the mind, not on the battlefield, he found himself an in-the-saddle soldier on a few unpleasant occasions.

One of thirteen children, Halleck grew up in New York State's Mohawk Valley. He graduated from West Point and taught French there for a year. (In that age, French was the language of war, not romance. West Point cadets studied French so they could read untranslated textbooks of military science.) Some of his writings impressed General Winfield Scott, who sent him to France to study military history.

Halleck went on to write military-science

textbooks and translate a French work on Napoleon's campaigns. He resigned from the army (one of the wisest decisions of his life, had he but stuck with it) to head the leading law firm in San Francisco during the gold rush. He also found time to write a book on international law. Wealthy at a fairly young age, he married Elizabeth Hamilton, the granddaughter of Alexander Hamilton, America's first treasury secretary and one of the authors of *The Federalist Papers*.

Things would have gone well for Old Brains (and for the Union army) had he stayed at his law office in San Francisco. Alas, when the war began, Halleck still believed he could make a name as a military leader. With Winfield Scott's backing, he was commissioned a major general and given a command in the West. At the beginning of the war, the armies lacked good topographical maps. Campaigning in the Western theater in 1862, Halleck found himself using maps he bought in a bookstore.

He received (and gladly took) credit for victories won by Grant and other generals. When Forts Donelson and Henry in Tennessee fell to the Union, Grant was the primary actor, but instead of praising him, Halleck pressed McClellan to arrest Grant for insubordination. Halleck based his request on the fact that communiqués he had sent to Grant

went unanswered. (The reason was that they never reached Grant.) Despite Grant's success, it was Halleck who told the War Department, "Give me the command in the West." He spent most of the war (and probably his remaining years) jealous of Grant. (One noted war correspondent observed that "gambling was the great vice of the men and jealousy was the great vice of the generals.")

In the field, Halleck could be slow as molasses. After the Battle of Shiloh, he took a command in Tennessee. After six weeks, he and his men arrived in Corinth, Mississippi. The Rebels were already fifty miles away. Halleck reported this as a victory.

Among the oddities of the Civil War was that in July 1862, Lincoln gave Old Brains the title of general in chief. In that position, he could voice his opinions about all the other generals, most of whom he disliked (and vice versa). Halleck was a stickler for detail and actually seemed to relish the writing of reports and dispatches. (This might explain his attraction to the French of the period, known for their tidy-mindedness and love of order.) An intellectual in his dealings with people, he had little ability to handle politicians and temperamental subordinates.

The man with the double chin had such loose skin that it jiggled when he talked. He

HENRY W.
HALLECK

1815–1872

had the disconcerting habit of looking side-ways at people when he spoke, and he was always nervously crossing his arms and scratching his elbows. And his fish-eyed stare was notorious. Someone called him "a vast emptiness surrounded by an education."

The man was rather pitiful. One senator asked Lincoln why he did not sack Halleck. Abe replied, "Well, the fact is, the man who has no friends should be taken care of." Lincoln said privately that Halleck was "little more than a first-rate clerk."

Then he found his niche. Once Lincoln pegged Grant as his fighting general and made him supreme commander of all Union armies, he gave Halleck a job he was good at: liaison to Grant. Halleck's title was chief of staff. He possessed the rare talent of being able to express military thought in civilian language (and civilian thought in military language), which

was of great use in communicating Lincoln's strategies to Grant. He saved the two from the miscommunication that had plagued Abe's relations with the high-strung George McClellan. Rather than writing directly to Lincoln, Grant sent dispatches to Halleck, who was also the liaison between Grant and the other chief generals. Joe Hooker sniped that Halleck, a general with no command, was like a man who married knowing he could not sleep with his wife. But the system of commander in chief, general in chief, and chief of staff did work.

It must have pained Old Brains to see Grant given command of all the Union armies. To Grant's credit, he never did gloat to his former superior. The fighter had risen above the clerk, which in war is the proper order of things.

Ambrose Powell Hill, Confederate General
(1825–1865)

CULPEPER'S PRIDE, IN CALICO

HE MAY BE THE ONLY Civil War general buried in the middle of an intersection. He may also be the only one whose health was ruined by gonorrhea. Considering that he had an almost perfect marriage, it is ironic that a youthful sexual indiscretion followed him throughout his life.

Powell Hill (as he was always called,

Southerners of that era often going by their middle names instead of their first) was one of seven children. He was devoted to his horse-loving father and his introverted, hypochondriac mother.

When he left Culpeper, Virginia, for West Point, his mother gave him a peculiar present: a small ham bone, which became the good-luck charm he carried all his life. And his schoolmaster gave him some old Latin advice: *Dulce et decorum est pro patria mori*—"Pleasant and fitting to die for one's fatherland." It was advice he was to follow.

At West Point, Powell introduced himself to a fellow Virginia boy, Thomas J. Jackson, later known as "Stonewall." Hill stated years later that "Jackson received me so coldly that I regretted my friendly overtures." The two never liked each other. In fact, during the war, they took an active *dislike* to each other, which caused their commander, Robert E. Lee, no end of grief.

Powell's roommate his first year at West Point was George McClellan, who was liked by everyone (at that time, anyway). None of McClellan's friends (and future Confederates) foresaw that he would one day command the Army of the Potomac, the enemy.

In September 1844, Powell was admitted to a clinic with gonorrhea he had contracted on a furlough—probably in New York City that summer. In those pre-penicillin days, there was no cure. You suffered and you got over it (or didn't). A minority of people kept it in their system, which caused below-the-waist difficulties throughout life. In a few weeks, Powell was sent home to recuperate. He had to repeat his third year at West Point. Throughout the rest of his life, he suffered from the malady,

sometimes in pure agony. When he died at age thirty-nine, he looked considerably older.

His classmates were ecstatic about the Mexican War, McClellan exulting, "War at last, sure enough! Ain't it glorious!" It was for Hill. In Mexico, he adopted a wild uniform: a flaming red flannel shirt, a huge sombrero, red-topped boots with enormous spurs, a saber, a butcher knife stuck in a wide belt. All in all, he was a well-armed bandito from the Old Dominion. (Years later, as a Confederate, Powell hardly looked "regulation" in uniform. He wore calico or checked shirts made by his wife, Dolly, boots almost hip high, and his trademark black felt hat and oversized buckskin gloves. A pipe was also part of his look.)

The war veteran fell in love with Ellen Marcy, who was pre-pre-engaged to his former roommate, McClellan. The Marcys were more enthusiastic than either Ellen or McClellan. While "Little Mac" was abroad, Hill sparked Ellen, and McClellan politely gave way. But the Marcys were horrified. Somehow, Ellen's mother found out that Hill had "the bad disease." Hill and the Marcys had a falling-out. Ellen sadly returned her engagement ring (inscribed with the words *Je t'aime*) to Hill. When she and Mac married, Hill was a groomsman. By that time, he had already wed his beloved Dolly.

When the Civil War broke out, the man

AMBROSE
POWELL
HILL

1825–1865

from Culpeper did the Virginia thing and re-signed his army commission. He had no par-ticular love for slavery or secession, but he loved Virginia.

He proved a ferocious fighter and one of the South's best generals. In precisely ninety days, he went from colonel of a regiment to major general of a division. Both Jackson (who still disliked him intensely) and Lee mentioned Hill's name in their last moments of life.

Hill was rightly proud of his accomplish-ments. But his commander, General James Longstreet, also had considerable pride. Fric-tion between the two began when the *Rich-mond Examiner* ran an article praising Hill and his men at the Battle of Frayser's Farm. Longstreet and his men's contributions were ignored. The peeved Longstreet wrote a re-buttal, which was published in a rival news-paper, the *Whig*. Longstreet claimed that the *Examiner* had exaggerated certain details of the Hill story. The proud Hill was angry enough to request that Lee remove him from Longstreet's command. Lee managed to resolve the difficulty, but two of his best generals by then despised each other.

Hill definitely had brass. One time, when Jefferson Davis placed himself too near the fire of a battle, Hill rode up and told both Davis and Lee, "This is no place for either of you, and as commander of this part of the field, I order you both to the rear!" Davis and Lee took it the right way. On another occasion, Hill caught a deserting captain hiding behind a tree. He cussed the man out and attempted to break his sword in half—but it only bent, being made of as bad a material as its possessor.

Hill's last word was "Surrender!" He died instantly from a Yankee bullet in the heart at Petersburg, just a few days before Lee surren-dered to Grant. The little redhead was wear-ing one of his trademark calico shirts and car-rying his mother's ham bone. Apparently, the good-luck charm had lost its power.

Postmortem: Hill's body had trouble find-ing its final resting place. His family buried him at its home. Then, two years later, some Confederate veterans reburied him at Richmond's Hollywood Cemetery, the "Arling-ton of Confederates." Twenty years after that, a Richmond developer (who was also a Con-federate veteran, naturally) wanted to lay out a new residential section with an A. P. Hill monument and grave as its centerpiece. In 1892, Hill's remains found their final (so far) resting place beneath a bronze statue—at the intersection of Laburnum and Hermitage in Richmond.

Daniel Harvey Hill, Confederate General
(1821–1889)

PROFESSOR SOUR

IN AN ERA when family ties were of vital importance, Harvey Hill (as he was always called) had a key connection: he was the brother-in-law of Thomas "Stonewall" Jackson. His adored and adoring wife, Isabella, was a sister of Jackson's adored and adoring Anna. The two men's connection went beyond family ties, since Hill helped steer the churchless Jackson into the Presbyte-

rian fold. Both men were devout Christians who loved God, their wives, and the South. And both were notably lacking in humor. If Jackson was dour, Hill was downright sour.

Why? Part of his sourness was physical. He had polio in his youth, which certainly affected his disposition. In his later years, he wrote, "I have a very feeble frame and have been a great sufferer from boyhood." (Jackson, who had no real physical problems to speak of, was a noted hypochondriac.)

Hill, one of eleven children, had a strict Presbyterian mother. She kept the Sabbath so devotedly (and joylessly) that his older brother John "took the blues on Thursday morning because Sunday was coming," according to Hill. The future general inherited from her a type of Christianity that gave life a solid moral foundation but brought little joy.

Like almost every other Civil War general, Hill had his baptism of fire in the Mexican War. Although he enjoyed fighting, he disliked the way the army was run, and he didn't mind telling people. While stationed at Fort Monroe in Virginia, he wrote a critique of the "ignorance and imbecility of the War Department," which he published under a pseudonym in a magazine. Had his identity been known, he would have been court-martialed. This set the pattern for his life: griping loud and long about his superiors (*not* the best way to win friends and influence people).

Bored with army life and unhappy with the low pay and frequent relocations, the waspish Hill took a job teaching math at Washington College in Lexington, Virginia, then at Davidson College in North Carolina. He published the textbook *Elements of Algebra*, notable for its problems in which Yankees

were made to look like fools and incompetents. (Hill strongly believed in the superiority of Southerners and was a strong supporter of states' rights.) He helped his brother-in-law, Jackson, obtain his teaching post at the Virginia Military Institute in Lexington.

Hill began the Civil War on a bright note: his men were victorious at the war's first major battle, Big Bethel in Virginia. (If not exactly a major battle, it was at least a major minor battle.) Hill was promoted to brigadier general and went on to fight in several battles under Robert E. Lee and Jackson. The cantankerous, stern-faced general was noted for bravery (some thought it recklessness). His men called him "Old Rawhide," which they didn't necessarily mean as a compliment. But he did have grit. Hill would sometimes expose himself to fire just to settle his men's nerves. He had a backbone of iron and a soul of vinegar.

Like many sour-tempered men, Hill had a sweet-natured wife who took some (but not all) of the venom out of his personality. His wartime letters to Isabella were full of grousing and sarcasm. Hill saw the gloomy side of everything, even things that should have gladdened him. In spite of the widespread religious revival among the Confederates, Hill the Christian had a pessimistic view of the whole thing: "Very few soldiers attend, and seem very

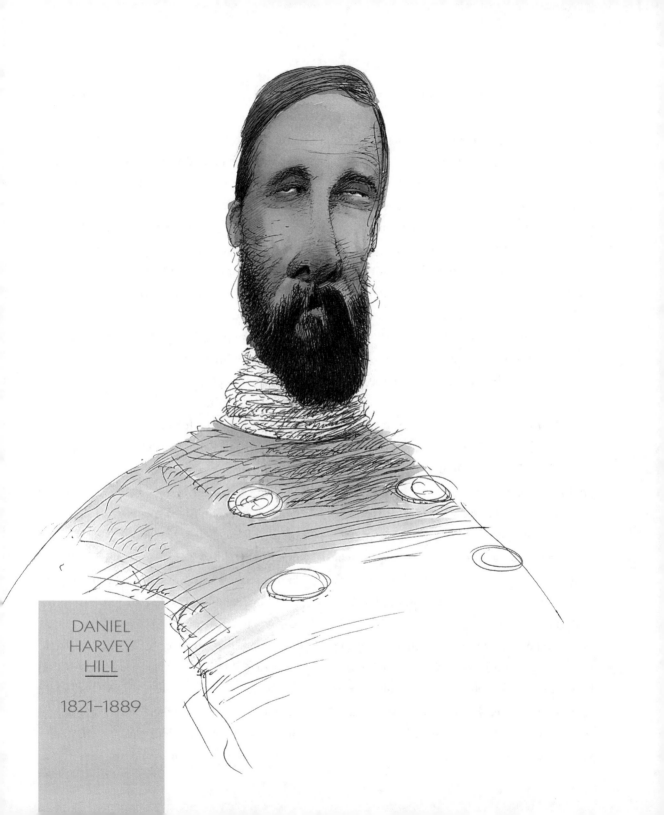

DANIEL
HARVEY
HILL

1821–1889

indifferent about their souls." He was mistaken; *lots* of men were caught up in the revival. He also had a low opinion of the chaplains in the Confederate army: "Our regimental chaplains are as trifling as the regimental surgeons, which is the strongest denunciation I can make." He criticized his own denomination, the Presbyterians, saying they were "remarkable for their piety, bigotry, hospitality, and intolerance."

Sometimes, his caustic writings were on target. On one occasion, he wrote his wife, "We have driven McClellan out of his fortifications. . . . Still he claims a great victory. The art of lying can go no farther." When one of his subordinates, political general Robert Toombs, challenged him to a duel, Hill wisely pointed out that they should spend their energy killing the enemy.

Hill groused constantly about the Confederate army's upper ranks. He criticized Lee (heaven forbid!) and sometimes even his own brother-in-law, Jackson. (The tactless man was not content to gripe in conversation, but stupidly put his beefs in writing—that is, in his official reports of battles.) Hill stated after the war that "General Jackson never spoke an unkind word to me, publicly or privately, at any time or any place." Probably true, since Jackson was notoriously tight-lipped. But the reverse was definitely not true: Hill said many,

many unkind words about Jackson. Both Lee and Jackson were pleased when Hill left the Army of Northern Virginia. The generals under Hill's command were also happy. One of them wrote his wife that Hill had been reassigned, "much to our delight."

After being reassigned, Hill's biggest mistake was in loudly and openly criticizing General Braxton Bragg, a friend and pet of President Jefferson Davis. In fact, practically everyone who served under Bragg criticized him, but Hill overstepped his bounds, and Bragg used his clout with Davis to have Hill removed from command (a case of one crab getting rid of another crab).

Postwar, the former general became a keeper of the flame for the Confederacy, editing the magazines *The Land We Love* and *The Southern Home*. And like so many Confederate generals, he published memoirs designed to polish his own halo (or, more accurately, to create one). He differed from other ex-Rebels in one sense: he never ceased to criticize Robert E. Lee, and so had no part in creating the postwar image of the saintly and all-wise Lee.

Hill was a textbook case of a particular kind of military leader, one whose grit and combativeness served well on the battlefield but were a hindrance when battle was not raging. He was far better in the role of soldier than in the role of human being.

John Bell Hood, Confederate General

(1831–1879)

TEXAS ROMEO ON CRUTCHES

BEFORE HE LOST his right leg and the use of his left arm, John Hood was considered quite a catch. He was six-foot-two, with sad blue eyes, a thick blond beard, reddish blond hair, broad shoulders, and a lovely voice. After the amputation of his leg following the Battle of Chickamauga, the thirty-two-year-old Hood became even

more of a catch, for he was then the Wounded Knight. On top of that, he was one of the few gallant generals who was still (amazingly) a bachelor.

The site of his recuperation was Richmond, where he became the toast of capital society. His heart's desire was a beautiful and haughty belle, Sally Buchanan

Preston, known as "Buck." She resisted (or pretended to resist) the general on crutches, and he enjoyed the chase. Buck refused Hood's proposals twice, then agreed to an engagement, despite her aristocratic family's objections. By the time of Hood's military disasters at Franklin and Nashville in 1864, the relationship had ended. Buck apparently could tolerate a handicapped man but not a failure.

Poor Hood! Early in the war, he was one of the South's most promising fighting men. The son of a Kentucky doctor, he was an 1853 West Point grad. For some reason lost to history, he became known as "Old Sam" at the academy and afterward. He graduated while Robert E. Lee was superintendent there, and Lee was fond of him.

While stationed in Texas, the tall Kentucky boy formed a deep attachment to the Lone Star State. The Virginia-fixated Lee spoke of Texas as a "desert of dullness," but some soldiers shared Hood's enthusiasm for its wide-open spaces. When Texas seceded, Hood headed to Richmond to volunteer his services. He rose rapidly in rank and was given the new Fourth Texas Infantry.

Hood had the same philosophy of war as Lee: Destroy, don't merely defeat. Though he commanded "Hood's Texas Brigade" for only six months, the men proudly called themselves

that name until the bitter end. Hood passed his intensity on to his men. Lee claimed they were the fiercest and most dependable troops in the Army of Northern Virginia. Hood disliked fighting from behind cover and believed that head-on attacks developed the fighting character.

Hood's Texans didn't give two hoots about military spit and polish. They were Confederate grunge, and proud of it. When they marched through Richmond, they impressed everyone with their scroungy look. Most of their clothing had been snatched from the enemy. Tin pans and pots were tied to their waists, and bread or bacon was stuck on the ends of their bayonets. When the ragged men marched through Chambersburg, Pennsylvania, well-dressed Yankee women jeered and laughed. One woman wore a Union flag defiantly on her bosom, which inspired one of Hood's men to tell her, "Take care, ma'am—Hood's boys are great at storming breastworks when the Yankee colors is on 'em." They had a footloose attitude toward private property even in Confederate territory. Robert E. Lee told Hood that "when you Texans come about, the chickens have to roost mighty high." Running short on headgear, Hood's boys solved the problem by knocking the hats off men on a slow-moving train.

JOHN
BELL
HOOD

1831–1879

Hood took a shot in his left arm at Gettysburg and never regained the use of it. He lost his right leg at Chickamauga. He was expected to die from the wound, but he slowly recuperated. The man with the double handicap was offered a civil post, but he refused. "No bombproof place for me," he said.

During his recovery, Old Sam found time not only to court Buck Preston but also to examine his soul. While on crutches, he was baptized by the Confederacy's "Fighting Bishop," General Leonidas Polk. The bishop-general performed the rite in Hood's tent late at night, to the sound of Federal cannon booming.

Jefferson Davis was in a quandary: What to do about Sherman's destructive march through Georgia? Joe Johnston, commander of the Army of Tennessee, was having no luck.

Davis did something that sent fear and trembling through the ranks: he changed generals in mid-campaign. Johnston was out, and Hood (who ached for the job) was in. The gritty general with one leg and a useless arm in a sling had to be strapped to his saddle, but he was raring for a fight. His appointment received mixed reviews. Lee wrote Davis, "Hood is a bold fighter. I am doubtful as to other qualities necessary."

Hood had a daring plan, which Davis approved. He would leave Georgia, head back to Tennessee, and strike the Union base at Nashville. This was supposed to be the bait that would draw Sherman out of Georgia. It didn't work. Hood laid siege to the city, but it was broken in December 1864 by George Thomas (formerly one of Hood's instructors at West Point). At his own request, Hood was relieved of command. Bits and pieces of his broken army drifted back toward the Gulf, singing a parody of "The Yellow Rose of Texas":

> *The gallant Hood of Texas*
> *Played hell in Tennessee.*

Some say that Hood's decision to march into Tennessee was the fatal military decision of the war. The Battle of Nashville was a debacle by any reckoning.

Postwar, Old Sam didn't manage to settle in Texas, as he had planned. He lived in New Orleans and married Anna Marie Hennen. It was a fertile marriage. His cotton business thrived, and they had eleven children, including three sets of twins. Hood took the time to pen his war memoirs, *Advance and Retreat*, which were as self-excusing (and other-accusing) as most Civil War memoirs. His book was prompted by the earlier self-excusing set of memoirs, those of Joe Johnston, the man Hood replaced in Georgia. Johnston and Hood went to their graves despising each other and blaming one another for the Army of Tennessee's defeat.

A final calamity befell Hood. In 1878 and 1879, a yellow fever epidemic struck New Orleans, which led to the closing of the cotton exchange—which in turn ruined Hood. He lost his wife and one daughter to the fever, then he himself died of it a few days later. His last words, spoken in the delirium of fever, were "I leave my children to the Texas Brigade." Unfortunately, he left no assets to support the ten orphans. Friends published Hood's memoirs and supported the children from the proceeds. The Confederacy's Texas Romeo died at age forty-eight.

Joseph Hooker, Union General
(1814–1879)

RICHMOND OR BUST

RUMOR HAS IT that prostitutes came to be called "hookers" because they were a vital part of General Hooker's camp followers. Actually, the word *booker* was around long before that. But the boastful, ambitious Union general did have a fondness for hookers. The man whose mother hoped he would be a minister preferred the "host-esses" at his favorite haunt, the Blue Wing Tavern. One critic claimed that while Hooker was in command, "the headquarters of the Army of the Potomac was a place to which no self-respecting man liked to go, and no decent woman could go. It was a combination of bar-room and brothel." It must have pleased the viceless and devout Stonewall Jackson that he defeated the boozy, poker-playing, womanizing Hooker so soundly at the Battle of Chancellorsville.

Hooker was ambitious as all get-out. During the war, he frequently prefaced his comments with "When I get to Richmond" or "After we have taken Richmond." President Lincoln was once heard to say, "That is the most depressing thing about Hooker. It seems to me that he is overconfident."

He was also brave. At Williamsburg in May 1862, he earned the nickname "Fighting Joe" for the fortitude he exhibited even after falling in the mud with his dying horse. He took a wound in the foot at Antietam but stayed in the saddle and on the field until the fighting was done. The press liked him in part because he was valiant, but also because he delighted in telling reporters what he thought of other officers. (Journalists adore mudslingers.)

After the Union's painful defeat at Fredericksburg, Hooker was one of several officers who complained about their superior, General Ambrose Burnside. The genial Burnside requested that either he or the griping officers be relieved. Lincoln chose to remove Burnside, replacing him with Hooker. One of Lincoln's cabinet members protested, for he had heard Hooker was a boozer—"too great a friend of John Barleycorn."

In a long letter in January 1863, Lincoln stated the obvious when he told the new commander, "What I ask of you is military success." Lincoln told him, "Beware of rashness, but with energy, and sleepless vigilance, go forward, and give us victories." Hooker had been heard to say that the Union army (and in fact the Union itself) needed a dictator. Presumably, he proposed himself for the post. But as Lincoln told him, "Only those generals who gain successes can set up dictators." Lincoln also accused him of thwarting his superior, Burnside, at every turn, all in the interest of his own ambition. Curiously, the self-flaunting Hooker appreciated this father-son letter and shed tears over it.

Fighting Joe rose to the challenge and worked to reorganize the demoralized Army of the Potomac. He claimed that the Union army was better than the Rebel army in every way but one: "in vigor of attack." Hooker blamed this on the army's former commander, McClellan, whom he called "a baby" (an accurate description) and a man "who knew something of drill, little of organization, and nothing of the morale of the army."

But at Chancellorsville, Hooker did a McClellanish thing in passing up a grand opportunity to attack when Lee was vulnerable. Before the battle, he boasted, "My plans are

JOSEPH
HOOKER

1814–1879

perfect. May God have mercy on General Lee, for I will have none." He also predicted (wrongly) that "God Almighty will not be able to prevent the destruction of the Rebel army." As it turned out, the battle was a severe blow for the Union, which suffered seventeen thousand casualties. Everyone blamed Hooker, who in turn laid the blame on the Eleventh Corps, which was composed mostly of Germans.

Fighting Joe seriously underestimated Lee, calling him a "courtier" who had earned his reputation by kissing up to General Winfield Scott. Likewise, Lee had no high opinion of Hooker, thinking him more talk than action, good at looking determined but basically indecisive.

Hooker just missed being in the grand battle of the war. Lincoln was exhilarated on learning of the Confederates' invasion of Pennsylvania, saying, "We cannot help beating them if we have the man. How much depends in military matters on one master mind!" Lincoln believed Fighting Joe could still be that man, but others were less confident. Then Hooker resigned, probably due to a lack of confidence in his own abilities (or to a lack of *others'* confidence in him). He was replaced by George Meade three days before Gettysburg. Would that fateful battle have gone differently had Fighting Joe still been in command? It makes for some amusing speculation.

Hooker was, many said, handsome as a Greek god—tall and well built, with a florid complexion, strawberry blond hair, and bright blue eyes. He had looks, ambition, even guts. But he never did get to Richmond.

Curiously, Hooker claimed he did not like his famous nickname. "Don't call me Fighting Joe," he said. "It makes the public think that I am a hotheaded, furious young fellow, accustomed to making furious and needless dashes at the enemy."

Thomas J. "Stonewall" Jackson, Confederate General
(1824–1863)

DEMON DEACON

STONEWALL JACKSON'S image is carved in granite on Georgia's Stone Mountain. That is appropriate, because the great general was in fact a stone face and a stiff—usually. Jackson was a cuddly cream puff with children and his adored wife, Anna ("my little pet dove," he called her), but a tight-lipped, humorless stuffed shirt with most everyone else. The poor man actually lacked the ability to laugh out loud. Witnesses said that on the rare occasions when he found something funny, he could only throw back his head and quiver—the motion of laughing without the sound, like a laugh in a silent movie.

Perhaps his sour demeanor was connected to his habit of sucking lemons. (Or so the legend goes. Apparently, someone saw Jackson sucking a lemon during a battle, and the story spread that he *always* had lemons—which was not the case.) He claimed he was a teetotaler because he liked liquor too much and feared becoming an addict. He frustrated hostesses by showing up at dinner parties with his own food—usually plain bread. Or he would dine at home on his strict, boring fare, then show up for dinner and only drink water. The poor hypochondriac was convinced that practically every sort of food gave him dyspepsia (the generic name for stomach troubles back then). He told one hostess, "The moment a grain of black pepper touches my tongue, I lose all strength in my right leg." He would have fit in well with today's food-and-fitness fanatics.

He was notoriously devout, so much so that some called him "Deacon" Jackson. After one dazzling battlefield victory, he dashed off a quick letter home that never mentioned the battle at all. Instead, he enclosed his regular contribution to his church's Sunday school and apologized for being late with it. Jackson took the Sabbath seriously and announced that Sunday was off-limits for war, although he could be persuaded to fight "more ordinary battles" on Sunday. (Meaning what? Lower body counts? Fewer pints of blood lost?) He had a longstanding feud with fellow Virginia general A. P. Hill, who called Jackson "that crazy old Presbyterian fool" but admitted the fool could fight. Jackson told his men, "My prayer is that this may be an army of the living God as well as of its country." (It is perhaps best left to the theologians to decide whether an army can be both.)

Deacon Jackson enjoyed belting out hymns in church. No one else enjoyed it, as Jackson was tone-deaf. On one occasion, he described the infamous Rebel yell as "the sweetest music I ever heard." Many Southerners agreed with him on that.

Prior to the war, Jackson taught (rather badly) at the Virginia Military Institute. Most of his students detested him both as a man and as a teacher. "Tom Fool" was one of the more polite nicknames the cadets bestowed on him. One student tried to drop a brick on Jackson's head. Another challenged him to a duel (a favorite Southern pastime in those days), which never materialized. In one of the war's many ironies, that student later fought under Jackson and became one of his ardent admirers. Professor Jackson did grow more animated when teaching his favorite subject, artillery (which happened to be the one subject in which he was genuinely qualified).

THOMAS J.
"STONEWALL"
JACKSON

1824–1863

Jackson the Christian made a hell of a soldier. At First Manassas, he earned his great *nom de guerre*, "Stonewall." Tight-lipped though he was, he ordered his soldiers, "Charge men, and yell like furies!" After First Manassas, while a surgeon dressed his wounded finger, Jackson said, "Give me ten thousand men, and I will be in Washington tomorrow." He was one of the bodacious success stories of the war, a strategist and disciplinarian who could invigorate his worn-out infantry into swift-moving "foot cavalry." He carried his battle plans only in his head, a source of endless frustration to other officers. He once stated, "If my hat knew my plans, I would burn it."

His guiding word in life was *duty*. He expected subordinates to do as they were told, and he was willing to do so himself, saying, "So great is my confidence in General Lee that I am willing to follow him blindfolded." The army couldn't argue with one basic fact: Jackson won battles. His combination of canny strategy and fearlessness was a constant vexation to the North. Yankee mothers could frighten their toddlers by saying, "Stonewall will get you!"

Jackson never played the role of elegant Southern cavalier. He clomped around in oversize boots (his feet were huge), rode a horse barely larger than a pony, and kept his cap pulled down so far that his eyes were barely visible. Still, those blue eyes had an almost demonic (or was it heavenly?) way of flashing when he was fired up. No wonder one of his nicknames was "Old Blue Light."

Being a God-fearing man, Jackson never sought glory for himself. It came anyway, but he was never comfortable with it. His friend (and polar opposite in personality), the dashing and gregarious Jeb Stuart, loved getting gifts from admirers. Jackson had more of an "Aw, shucks" attitude. He wrote his wife regarding press coverage of his victories, "Don't trouble yourself about representations that are made of me. These things are earthly and transitory. There are real and glorious blessings for us beyond this life." But the compliments came nonetheless, and in many forms. A captured Yankee soldier was once caught plucking hairs out of Jackson's horse's tail. Jackson asked him why, and the soldier doffed his hat and said respectfully, "General, each one of those hairs is worth a dollar in New York." Not being a glory-seeker himself, Jackson did not gush compliments for others. His highest praise for anyone was "Very commendable, very commendable." Once, when told that one of his messengers had been killed, he murmured (without thinking), "Very commendable."

His lack of humor was notorious. Jeb

Stuart had a German officer, Heros von Borcke, who admired Jackson greatly. The German, whose English was less than perfect, once attempted to say, "It warms my heart when he talks to me," but it came out, "It makes my heart burn when he talks to me." When he told Jackson, the amused Stuart further translated the line as "It gives me heartburn when he talks to me." Jackson could not understand why everyone was laughing.

After the smashing victory at Chancellorsville, Jackson was hit by friendly fire. His wounded left arm was amputated and buried reverently. Earlier, the general had said, "God has fixed the time of my death. I do not concern myself about that, but to be always ready." No doubt, he was. His wife brought their infant daughter, Julia, to his deathbed, and Jackson, floating in and out of delirium, stroked her head with his remaining hand and said, "Sweet one! Little comforter!" The devout Presbyterian lingered a few days, then died (as he wished) on a Sunday. His final words—"Let us cross over the river and rest under the shade of the trees"—became some of the most quoted of the Civil War. The Confederacy went into mourning. Once he was dead, his oddities were forgotten, and the peculiar Tom Fool became the mighty Stonewall of legend.

One of the people deeply grieved at Jackson's passing was the devoted Jim Lewis, his black servant. The historians aren't quite sure whether Lewis was Jackson's slave or whether Jackson "hired him out" from someone else. Whatever his status, Lewis dearly loved "de Gen'ral."

Ulysses S. Grant, visiting the small house where Stonewall died, summed up the sentiment of South, North, and posterity perfectly: "He was a gallant soldier and a Christian gentleman." The house in Caroline County, Virginia, is now the Stonewall Jackson Shrine.

Jackson's face appeared on the Confederacy's largest unit of currency, the five-hundred-dollar note. He was the only deceased person pictured on Confederate bills.

Andrew Johnson, Union Politician
(1808–1875)

FOLLOWING THE TOUGH ACT

TWO THINGS Johnson always wore: a re-
volver in his right hip pocket and a hatred
for aristocrats. It was because of the second that he needed the first.

Johnson came from the same working-
class, self-educated background as Abe Lincoln. Young Andy was apprenticed to a tailor. In the shop, he picked up the rudiments
of reading and writing. (Or so says one

story. The other is that his beloved wife,
Eliza, whom he married when she was sixteen, taught him to read and write.) He
ran away from his domineering master and
settled in Greeneville in hilly East Tennessee, very much a frontier region, where he
ran a tailor shop and entered local politics. He was an alderman, then mayor,
then a Tennessee legislator. From 1843

to 1853, he served in Congress, where he met Abe Lincoln.

Johnson represented people like himself—workers and small farmers—and practically no slave owners. The tailor-politician hated slavery not because it was inhumane and un-Christian (the Northern abolitionist argument) but because he detested slave-holding aristocrats. He believed they despised common whites as much as they despised slaves.

But to expand his voting base statewide, he took a stand (or appeared to) for the rights of slave owners, which helped him get elected governor, then United States senator. In the 1860 presidential race, he was for Southern Democrat John Breckinridge. Johnson was proslavery for political reasons but pro-Union out of conviction: he did not believe in secession. When other Southerners resigned from the Senate, he and they exchanged heated words. As the only Southern senator to remain, he became a hero in the North—a Southern working man with no love of slavery or secession.

Tennessee was not anxious for secession, but after the firing on Fort Sumter and Lincoln's call for troops, the state did secede, and Johnson became *persona non grata* in his homeland. In Greeneville, the Confederates gave Eliza thirty-six hours to vacate the family's home. She stubbornly insisted she needed more time (and ultimately took five months before she joined her husband).

By 1862, an odd situation developed. Nashville and most of Middle Tennessee (there is no *central* Tennessee, as all Tennesseans know) was occupied by the Union, while East Tennessee and its mostly pro-Union population was held by the Confederacy. Lincoln made the loyal Johnson military governor of the state (the part occupied by the Federals, that is), hoping to establish a pro-Union government.

Johnson found his state difficult to manage. Even its Union people were proslavery, and they saw Johnson as (horrors!) a radical. In the fall of 1862, he endorsed recruiting runaway slaves as soldiers. This riled Unionists and turned them against Johnson and Lincoln. As *Harper's Weekly* noted, "Of Andrew Johnson it is enough to say that there is no man in the country, unless it be Mr. Lincoln himself, whom the Rebels more cordially hate."

Unpopular in Tennessee, Johnson did speaking tours in the North, where he was warmly received. He was the South's "Mr. Union," and the Republicans shrewdly nominated him as Lincoln's running mate in 1864. The party was, for that one election only, the "Union Party," not the Republican.

ANDREW
JOHNSON

1808–1875

The Republicans were trying to shed their image as a party of the North only.

Johnson became vice president in March 1865. He was quite visibly drunk (from brandy) at the inauguration and made what one observer called a "maudlin, drunken speech." One cabinet member commented, "Johnson is either drunk or crazy." In his speech, he rambled on about his common-folk roots and reminded the dignitaries of the Supreme Court and the cabinet that they were "creatures of the people" (valid sentiments, but expressed crudely and drunkenly). Someone asked Lincoln what would happen to the country if he were suddenly "removed" and Johnson became president. Lincoln replied, "I have known Andy for many years. He made a bad slip . . . but you need not be scared. Andy ain't a drunkard."

Five weeks later, following Lincoln's assassination, he was president. He barely missed being killed himself. John Wilkes Booth's fellow assassin George Atzerodt got cold feet and did not kill Johnson as planned.

Before Lincoln's death, Johnson had talked tough about hanging Jefferson Davis and other leading Rebels. (Johnson nursed a grudge against Davis from their days in Congress together. Davis once made some slighting remark about tailors, and Johnson took it per-sonally and believed Davis's apology was insincere.) But the tough talk was mostly wind. Johnson did despise Southern aristocrats, but not the whole South, since it had (so he believed) been led into the war by its plantation lords. He knew that the Radical Republicans in Congress might actually execute the Rebel leaders, and worse. He was convinced they would scrap the Constitution in order to ride roughshod over the South.

As Lincoln would have done, Johnson pursued a fairly lenient Reconstruction. But he lacked Lincoln's tact. He used language so violently and hastily that some thought him mad. He had the emotional self-control (or lack thereof) of a frontier boy, which was exactly what he was. (Mary Chesnut referred to him as "the drunken tailor" and "Andy, made Lord of all by the madman Booth." Mary Lincoln referred to him as "that miserable inebriate.")

Inevitably, he locked horns with a North-ern-dominated Radical Republican Congress bent on plaguing the former Confederacy as long as possible. The grand Radical in his cabinet was Secretary of War Edwin Stanton. Johnson sacked the bitter old bully, but Congress had passed the Tenure of Office Act (over Johnson's veto—one of his *many* vetoes), which prohibited the president from firing members of his own cabinet. The Senate licked its lips at finding an excuse for impeachment. The vote in May 1868 for removing Johnson from office fell one vote shy. To no one's surprise, Johnson was not the Republican candidate in 1868.

Greeneville, Tennessee, still has the home, tailor shop, and grave of its most famous son. The locals prefer to remember Andy Johnson for positive, noncontroversial things—like purchasing Alaska.

Albert Sidney Johnston, Confederate General
(1803–1862)

THE SOUTH'S GREAT WHAT-IF

SOLDIERS ARE PRONE to gripe, and one of the biggest gripes of Civil War soldiers was that the generals were "bombproofs" who directed the killing but did not often risk death themselves. But 'tweren't so, for many generals died in the war. In fact, of all American wars, the Civil War saw the highest percentage of generals die from battle wounds. Some of them were the brightest and best. The most famous victim was Stonewall Jackson, but the Confederacy suffered an earlier loss of one of its stars—the renowned Albert Sidney Johnston.

Johnston fit everyone's idea of what a general should look like. He was a big man, over six feet and over two hundred pounds, well built. Like any good Southern gentleman, he was also charming and courteous. And unlike most generals, he even had a sense of humor.

And Lord knows he had experience— more than any other Confederate general, in fact. Johnston was a general in Texas's war for independence from Mexico; he also served as the secretary of war under Sam Houston, the president of the Republic of Texas. Johnston was a distinguished colonel in the Mexican War, Robert E. Lee serving as his second in command. The formidable Winfield Scott called him "a Godsend to the army and to his country." Johnston also fought in the Black Hawk War and in that neglected bit of American history, the Mormon War of 1857.

But where the new nation known as the Confederate States of America was concerned, Johnston had an even more important qualification: President Jefferson Davis had idolized him for years. Davis knew Johnston from their days at Transylvania University in Kentucky, one of America's most respected colleges in the 1800s (though its name had nothing to do with vampires). And Johnston was two years ahead of Davis at West Point. After the war, Davis recalled, "I hoped and expected that I had others who would prove generals, but I knew I had one, and that was Sidney Johnston." Davis called him "the greatest soldier, the ablest man, civil or military, Confederate or Federal, then living." (Given such impossibly high expectations, perhaps it's well that Johnston met the fate he did.)

Like Davis, Johnston was a Kentucky boy, but he relished his Texas days and adopted the Lone Star State as his home. When Texas seceded in 1861, he declined an offer of high rank in the Union army. Along with a group of other pro-Southern officers, he shipped off to New Orleans, then on to Richmond by train. Davis made him a full general (one of the first in the Confederacy) and offered him the command of the Western Department.

That was a challenge. Johnston had the daunting task of defending a line running from Kentucky across Arkansas into Indian territory, crossed by the Mississippi, Tennessee, and Cumberland Rivers. (In Confederate contexts, the *West* referred to Tennessee, Alabama, Mississippi—and everything farther west.) Besides defending that vast chunk of earth, poor Johnston had to make do with such buffoon generals as John Floyd and Gideon Pillow, who lost Forts Donelson and Henry in Tennessee to a rising Union star named U. S. Grant.

Grant's successes in Tennessee were sledgehammer blows to Confederate morale, and there was an outcry in the South that

ALBERT
SIDNEY
JOHNSTON

1803–1862

Jefferson Davis sack Johnston. Davis stood by his old friend (this was one of Davis's better qualities), believing there was no better man to put in his place.

Not long afterward in Tennessee, Johnston encountered Grant himself at a fateful battle called Shiloh, fought April 6 and 7, 1862, and named for a small Methodist church at the battle site.

At the peach orchard at Shiloh, Johnston gave his men a hearty pep talk, telling them to use their bayonets. He rose in his stirrups, waved his hat, and cheered them forward, crying, "I will lead you!"—hardly the words of a "bombproof." The men drove the Yanks out of the orchard. Johnston came riding back, all smiles, but bystanders noticed his uniform and one boot had been ripped by bullets. Then he reeled in his saddle.

One of his aides, Tennessee governor Isham Harris, rushed to him and asked, "General, are you hurt?"

"Yes, and I fear seriously."

Harris led horse and rider to a secluded place, where he began checking Johnston for wounds. He saw that the general's right boot was full of blood. A bullet had pierced his knee and severed the femoral artery. Alas, Harris didn't know that a tourniquet might have stopped the bleeding. Johnston's own staff doctor was not at hand, for the general had sent him to look after some wounded among the captured, saying, "These men were our enemies a moment ago. They are our prisoners now. Take care of them."

The grief-stricken Harris could see the general was fading fast. "Johnston, do you know me?" he asked.

But the general had already died. His compassion for his wounded enemies had led to his own death. The gritty Kentuckian had remarked before the battle, "I would fight them if they were a million." The Yankees weren't that many, but one stray minie ball in an artery was sufficient.

Johnston has gone down in history as a great what-if, since no one knows how events in the western Confederacy might have played out if he had lived. Shiloh was a Union victory but also a personal setback for U. S. Grant, since Johnston's surprise attack led to his temporary eclipse. The battle was also a victory of sorts for Johnston's subordinate, the egotistical P. G. T. Beauregard. The Confederacy had sent the vain and overeager Beauregard west under Johnston to deflate his ego (Beauregard didn't like to be *under* anyone). But ironically, Johnston was killed and the Rebels at Shiloh came under the command of Beauregard.

One of Johnston's biographers called him the "Soldier of Three Republics," since he served the armies of the United States, the Republic of Texas, and the Confederate States of America. He was the Confederacy's only full general (four stars, that is) to die in battle. Texans certainly thought well of him, as evidenced by his grave in the Texas State Cemetery in Austin, one of the most elaborate tombs of any Confederate.

A postwar note: the general's son, Colonel William Preston Johnston, joined other Civil War veterans to help establish the national battlefield and cemetery at Shiloh, the site where his father died.

Joseph E. Johnston, Confederate General
(1807–1891)

GRIEVANCEMASTER GENERAL

AT HIS BEST, he looked every inch a military commander, the distinguished Uncle Joe. Some said he resembled a gamecock—small in size but plucky and ready to fight. Too bad for the Confederacy that he wasn't much of a fighter.

Johnston, one of many Virginia boys high in the Confederacy, was a good friend of Lee. The friendship was an inheritance, for Johnston's father had served under Lee's father, Lighthorse Harry Lee, in the Revolution. Joseph E. and Robert E. graduated in the same West Point class, its only Virginians. Historians enjoy speculating that, though the two were friends, Johnston was jealous of Lee. But for a brief moment in

1860, Johnston outranked Lee—he was a brigadier general and Lee a lieutenant colonel.

Things changed quickly when both men found themselves in the army of that new nation, the C.S.A. Both turned down Lincoln's offer of commanding the Union armies. Both began as major generals in Virginia. Then it was decided that only one was needed—Lee. Johnston was reduced to brigadier general.

But the gamecock was doing fine. He was the commander of Confederate forces at First Manassas, a smashing victory that garnered him much praise. It led to President Jefferson Davis making him a full general, along with four others. But he wasn't pleased that he ranked fourth among the five.

Uncle Joe wouldn't let the matter lie. He exchanged catty letters with Davis and other Confederate officials not only about his rank but about military policy in general. Whether he liked it or not, Johnston became the center of the widening circle of people who had a beef with Davis. In her highly readable Civil War diary, Mary Chesnut referred to Johnston as the "polar star" of the anti-Davis clique. She said he was "such a good hater, it is a pity he had not elected to hate somebody else than the president of our country."

The reality of war intervened in a dramatic way when Uncle Joe was seriously wounded at Seven Pines, Virginia. With him out of commission for several months, and with Lee chalking up one victory after another, the question of who should outrank whom became less meaningful.

When he recovered, he was sent to the Confederate West (Mississippi and Tennessee, that is), an area in sore need of a wise commander. Johnston wasn't as wise as hoped. He proved himself incapable of aiding the besieged river city of Vicksburg, Mississippi. The city's fall was a blow to Southern morale, and Uncle Joe and Davis were even more at each other's throats. Johnston, hoping to lay the blame for the Vicksburg fiasco on Davis, fed information to such noted Davis haters as Senator Louis Wigfall. On one occasion, Wigfall told some friends, "Make Joe Johnston dictator and all will be well."

Davis probably would have been pleased to see Johnston remain in Mississippi (or somewhere even hotter), but he needed his services because of another troublesome general, Braxton Bragg. Uncle Joe replaced Bragg as commander of the Army of Tennessee. Everyone believed that anyone or anything would be better than Bragg, and Johnston was, at least in terms of building morale. But he and the president continued their nasty exchanges. And Johnston had no luck at all in keeping

JOSEPH E.
JOHNSTON

1807–1891

the Yankees out of Georgia. (Like Union general George McClellan, Johnston always hesitated to attack until he was sure he had enough men—and he hardly ever did.) An exasperated Davis replaced him with General John Hood. There was another reason behind Johnston's sacking: he had criticized Davis one too many times. To one of the president's representatives, he said, "Davis tried to do what God failed to do. He tried to make a soldier of Braxton Bragg, and you know the result. It couldn't be done." Eight days later, Davis replaced Johnston with Hood.

For months, Uncle Joe was a general without an army. Then Lee, who had been named general in chief, requested that Davis have Johnston assume command of the armies in the Carolinas. Johnston had no better luck there than Lee did in Virginia. He surrendered his armies to Sherman on April 26, 1865, at Bentonville, North Carolina—the war's "second Appomattox." Again, even in the order of surrender, he stood in Lee's shadow. Ironically (or perhaps appropriately), when the magnificent Lee statue was dedicated on Richmond's Monument Avenue in 1890, with a crowd of a hundred thousand or more watching, it was Joe Johnston who unveiled it. There stood the aged Uncle Joe—underneath a towering bronze Robert E. Lee.

Having spent most of the war feeling unappreciated, Uncle Joe became one of the many generals to write self-serving memoirs. For many years, historians took his memoirs at face value and rated him highly. But lately (fashions coming and going in history as in other things), Johnston has come to be seen as the quarrelsome and sometimes good commander he truly was.

Robert E. Lee, Confederate General
(1807–1870)

GENERAL DUTY

BEFORE THE GRAY-BEARDED god-patriarch was known as "Marse Robert" and the "Marble Man," he was "Granny Lee" and the "King of Spades." He had his detractors, as do most seemingly perfect people. Lee stated—or may have stated, for historians disagree—that *duty* was "the most sublime word in the English language." Perhaps the skeptics were irked that the great and dutiful man actually was as great and dutiful as he seemed.

Great men have things in common. William Shakespeare was born in Stratford on Avon; Robert Edward Lee was born in Stratford on the Potomac. (It's actually Stratford Hall, and the plantation and home are still there, open to the public.) Lee was well aware that his birthplace was only a few miles downriver from that of the big man himself, George Washington. Lee's father, the wayward but gallant Lighthorse Harry Lee, counted it his crowning honor that he was a friend of Washington. Young Robert grew up with Washington as his role model.

The Washington connection became even closer when Robert married Mary Custis, the great-granddaughter of Martha Washington. The heiress brought several estates to the marriage, including America's best-known and most-visited plantation, Arlington. He and Mary produced seven children in fourteen years. It would be an exaggeration to say he was henpecked, but he generally did whatever his wife asked. She always referred to him as "Mr. Lee."

Mr. Lee, the "Marble Man," was human. He liked to have his children tickle his feet. He would place his bare feet in their laps, and when they asked him to tell them a story, he would say, "No tickling, no story!"

Like his father and Washington, Lee was destined to be a soldier. He was second in his class at West Point. (There seems to be a curse of anonymity on whoever is first in his West Point class, the second-place men having always fared better.) Lee had zero demerits on his record.

Like most of the key players in the Civil War, Lee had the Mexican War as an internship. He distinguished himself in Mexico and served on the staff of the formidable Winfield Scott. Scott later referred to Lee as "the best soldier I ever saw in the field." Lee won some glory but saw the dark side of the military, too. From Mexico, he wrote his son Custis, "You have no idea what a horrible sight a field of battle is."

Other horrors were looming. The South was talking secession, but Lee wanted no part of it. He believed in the gradual emancipation of the slaves, which he said would occur inevitably "through the mild and melting influence of Christianity." (He owned a few slaves himself, some of whom he freed to settle in Liberia in Africa.)

He was wrong about the prospects of gradual emancipation. In 1859, he was sent to Harpers Ferry with the marines to capture the abolitionist terrorist John Brown. Following that, it was obvious that the slavery question would never be settled in a "mild and melting" fashion. Lee watched in agony, wondering if his beloved Virginia would secede, as other Southern states had done. It did. Considering his family's (and George Washington's) attachment to the Old Domin-

ROBERT E.
LEE

1807–1870

ion, he threw in his lot with his native state.

Curiously, Lee could have had command of the *Northern* armies. Lincoln, through Scott, offered him the United States armies after the firing on Fort Sumter. Lee declined. Instead, he accepted the command of Virginia's defenses and became a trusted adviser to Confederate president Davis.

In one of his first assignments, Lee provoked criticism. Sent to fortify Charleston (Lee was an engineer), he earned the unflattering title "King of Spades." A gentleman to the core, but one who didn't fear breaking a sweat, Lee learned that other highborn soldiers viewed the pick-and-shovel routine as beneath them. Trench digging, they believed, was for slaves and white trash.

Early in the war, he made no impression as a field commander. He was pretty much forced to abandon western Virginia to the Federals. Skeptics called him "Granny Lee" and claimed he was relying on the Lee name and his classy appearance, not on his ability as a fighter. Some thought him a paper shuffler in the Confederate bureaucracy.

But he soon began to prove his worth in the field. One victory followed another. Soldiers forgot "Granny Lee" and the "King of Spades" and saw the handsome, genteel Lee as an undefeatable god. He was Mars with manners. He never boasted, was quick to praise others, and give credit to God. Yet he did like war. After the smashing victory at Fredericksburg, he told another general, "It is well that war is so terrible—we should grow too fond of it!" Chancellorsville was another grand victory, though it resulted in the loss of Stonewall Jackson to friendly fire. The victorious Rebels hailed Lee with wild shouting. He had defeated an army more than twice the size of his.

Such victories were tough to follow. Lee's invasion of the North was foiled when the plans fell into the hands of the Federals. The infamous "Lost Order" caused the Confederacy no end of grief. It resulted in the gore of Antietam. Later came the debacle at Gettysburg. Lee wrote his wife, "Our success at Gettysburg was not so great as reported." His understatement was incredible—it was the Confederacy's worst defeat! In fact, there was amazing incompetence on the Confederate side (enough to keep historians busy even today). Lee accepted the blame for Gettysburg. But after the war, the South couldn't accept the saintly Lee's assessment and so laid the blame on every other Confederate present.

Worse followed in 1864, when Sherman's march through Georgia sapped Confederate morale. Lee shifted his attention to defending

Richmond, then was forced to flee west, hoping in desperation to link up with Joseph Johnston's army in North Carolina. He never got that far. At Appomattox in April 1865, he met the star of the U.S. military, U. S. Grant. He surrendered the Army of Northern Virginia (a name he had bestowed) to Grant, who courteously allowed Lee's men to keep their horses and return home peacefully. Contrary to the famous painting of the surrender, Lee and Grant never sat at a table facing each other.

After the war, many former Confederate leaders went into politics. Lee had no interest in this, nor in praising himself (and condemning others) by writing war memoirs. He accepted a post as president of small, struggling Washington College in Lexington, Virginia, for a salary of fifteen hundred dollars a year. He breathed life into the school (now Washington and Lee University). While there, he created the first department of journalism at an American college. (Ironically, he constantly frustrated journalists by refusing to discuss the war.)

Lee died on October 12, 1870. He was mourned in both the South and the North. His last words, appropriate for a soldier, were "Strike the tent." He was buried in the Lee Chapel at the college. Nearby is the grave of the Confederacy's "first horse," Lee's beloved Traveller (originally named Greenbrier).

After his death, the Lee legend grew (aided by the fact that he was darn near perfect). He did have a few detractors. One of his generals, D. H. Hill, wrote that "the vanity of the Virginians has made them glorify their own prowess and deify Lee." Probably true, but Lee himself was not vain at all. U. S. Grant claimed that Lee was never defeated but simply "overwhelmed." Military men across the world still think of him as a most amazing man.

Maybe the best tribute came from the men in the ranks. On one occasion, some soldiers were discussing a controversial new book, Darwin's *Origin of Species*. One soldier announced, "Boys, the rest of us may have developed from monkeys, but I tell you none less than God could have made such a man as Marse Robert."

Abraham Lincoln, Union President
(1809–1865)

ONE WAR, SO MANY ENEMIES

IS THERE ANYTHING new to be said about America's sixteenth president? Certainly, he has fascinated Americans (and foreigners as well) more than any other chief executive. The basic points of his story are old hat: his birth in a log cabin, his youthful days as a rail splitter, his career as a shrewd country lawyer, his folksy humor and anecdotes, his famous debates with Stephen Douglas, his candidacy as a "black Republican" in 1860, his call for volunteers to put down "the Southern insurrection," his search for a competent commanding general, the Emancipation Proclamation, the Gettysburg Address, his second inaugural address, his assassination by Booth in Ford's Theatre on Good Friday in 1865, just days after Lee's surrender at Appomattox.

No novelist or screenwriter could have invented such a compelling story or leading character. What is often overlooked in the Lincoln saga is that *he was not in his own lifetime the beloved statesmen, martyr, and saint that subsequent generations have honored.* During his brief time in Washington, Lincoln was reviled as no other president before or after. While the South hated him for reasons too obvious to mention, the North was just as spiteful, the public, journalists, politicians, his own cabinet, and his own party hurling one insult after another. The lanky man won the election of 1860 with 40 percent of the vote, but oh, what a price he paid.

First, he displeased the abolitionists and the Radicals in his own Republican Party. They hoped (and Southerners assumed) that Lincoln would free the slaves instantly on taking office. No dice. Though he is remembered as the "Great Emancipator," Lincoln disliked the hard-line stance of the abolitionists. The famous newspaper editor Horace Greeley, eager for emancipation, published an open letter, "The Prayer of Twenty Millions," which accused Lincoln of being "strangely and disastrously remiss" in not affirming that the war

was being fought to abolish slavery. Shortly afterward, Lincoln issued a reply in which he affirmed, "My paramount object in this struggle is to save the Union, and is not either to save or destroy slavery. If I could save the Union without freeing any slave, I would do it; and if I could save it by freeing all the slaves, I would do it." Abolitionist Wendell Phillips gave a widely reported speech in which he accused Lincoln of "serving the South." Lincoln, at least until the Emancipation Proclamation, impressed the abolitionists as either halfhearted or just too darn slow.

Then there was the clergy, skeptical of the man who quoted the Bible more than any other president (having read it since childhood) but who never formally joined a church and was probably not, in the traditional sense, a Christian. Never mind that Lincoln's sexual morals were above reproach (no extramarital flings, the old tale of his dalliance with Ann Rutledge being mostly legend). The clergy was displeased with Lincoln's reputation for telling smutty stories (though today none of them would even raise an eyebrow). On top of that, he enjoyed the theater. In those days of G-rated plays, some ministers considered the stage frivolous at best, immoral at worst.

Another group of critics—and these did have a legitimate gripe—saw him running roughshod over the Constitution. When a president takes office, he swears to uphold the Constitution. Lincoln took that oath seriously—*but* he saw the secession of the Southern states as a crisis that called for emergency measures. So to clamp down on pro-South traitors, he assumed powers that no president before or since has claimed. In late April 1861, he authorized raids on every telegraph office in the North, seizing originals and copies of all telegraphs sent or received in the previous year. With those as evidence, or even just the word of an informer, he had men taken from their homes in the dead of night and thrown in jail without explanation. He denied writs of habeas corpus, including those issued by the Supreme Court. He once told Congress, "It became necessary for me to choose whether I should let the government fall into ruin, or whether, availing myself of the broader powers conferred by the Constitution in cases of insurrection, I would make an effort to save it." Congress deferred grudgingly. But even good friends like Secretary of the Navy Gideon Welles were uncomfortable with Abe's willingness to throw civil liberties out the window.

Southerners, of course, despised him, referring to him as the "Gorilla Tyrant" and smearing both his looks and his footloose attitude toward the Constitution. Lincoln was accustomed to insults about his looks. When he was once accused of hypocrisy, he replied, "If I were two-faced, would I be wearing this one?" At six-foot-four, he never weighed more than 180 pounds. His feet were size fourteen, making it a task to buy shoes.

Later generations have thought him a superb speaker, but his homespun eloquence was mostly lost on his listeners. The famous Gettysburg Address is a case in point. Governor Curtin of Pennsylvania invited Lincoln to the dedication of Gettysburg National Cemetery as an afterthought. (General George Meade had been invited to speak but declined.) The governor asked Lincoln to make "a few appropriate remarks" after the real speech by noted orator Edward Everett, who prattled on for two hours. Lincoln's brief but timeless speech did not impress many. Congressional powerhouse Thaddeus Stevens sniped about Lincoln's being asked to appear at Gettysburg, saying, "Let the dead bury the dead." Stevens and many of his congressional colleagues believed Lincoln was politically washed up. Lincoln himself underrated his words at Gettysburg: "That speech won't scour. It is a flat failure."

And of course, people in both the North and the South criticized his working-class origins. Americans have a two-sided approach to

ABRAHAM
LINCOLN

1809–1865

people like Lincoln. They applaud the common man whose brains and character elevate him to high office, but once he is there, they sneer at his lack of polish. The East Coast snobs never let up in their condescension toward the self-educated Western man and his frumpy wife.

Relentless criticism takes its toll. Throughout his life, Lincoln was subject to what we call depression, though in those days, it was known as melancholy or even hypochondria—"hypo" for short. After the Union loss at Fredericksburg, Lincoln said, "If there is a worse place than hell, I am in it." After the Rebel victory at Chancellorsville, he sobbed, "My God, my God, what will the country say?" Those were only two of a multitude of depression-inducing setbacks. His proneness to "the blues" (his own expression) was probably at the root of his love for humor. He irked and puzzled his cabinet by taking time at meetings to read from such humorists as Petroleum V. Nasby and Orpheus C. Kerr. (Lincoln was at least lucky in having the funniest political satirists on his side.)

Perhaps because he drew so much criticism, Abe (a name he hated being called, by the way) was kind to other people under fire. He was particularly protective toward the general after his own heart, U. S. Grant. At war's

end, Grant was a national hero, but during the war itself, his favor rose and fell depending on the public's mood. At one point, the editor of the *Cincinnati Commercial* called him "a jackass in the original package . . . a poor drunken imbecile. . . . Grant will fail miserably, hopelessly, eternally." When Lincoln saw that letter, he responded, "I think General Grant has hardly a friend left, except myself." After the surrender of Vicksburg, a gleeful Lincoln said, "Grant is my man, and I am his the rest of the war!" Had it not been for John Wilkes Booth's derringer, the Lincoln-Grant friendship might have endured much longer.

Abe's former law partner, William Herndon, said that Lincoln had "cold" intelligence, that he was not subject to idealism or illusion when it came to sizing up human beings: "He saw things through a perfect mental lens. . . . He was not impulsive, fanciful, or imaginative, but cold, calm, and precise." Yet while most such men are hard-boiled cynics, Lincoln wasn't. The man liked human beings, warts and all. His phrase "with malice toward none" wasn't just a pretty sentiment but his true stance.

The horrible and divisive period we call Reconstruction would surely have been less of a trial had the lanky Illinois lawyer lived to guide it.

Mary Todd Lincoln, Union First Lady
(1818–1882)

HELLCAT AND FLOWER CHILD

"MRS. PRESIDENT" was what General George McClellan called Abraham Lincoln's wife. He didn't mean it affectionately. The marriage of Abe and Mary Lincoln was a classic case of a genial, humorous man bonded to a shrill, temperamental woman.

In most ways, they were a mismatch. Mary Todd had been a belle in the Illinois capital of Springfield. The Todds had money and name, and the academy-educated Mary spoke fluent French. When she met Abraham Lincoln, he lost his head for her, impressed by her sophistication, her breeding, and her occasional flashes of temper. At five-foot-two, she was fourteen inches shorter than Abe. She was called "fashionably plump" in an age that did not worship thinness in women.

The governor of Illinois told Mary she was throwing herself away, since she and the bumpkin Lincoln were of different classes. Her own family mocked Abe's frontier accent. But Mary was less snobbish than they. She was a climber and thought Lincoln had a future.

Lincoln had misgivings and stood Mary up at the altar, attributing it to "nerves." A romance-minded editor's wife invited Mary and Abe to a party and urged them to "be friends again." Abe gave Mary a plain gold ring inscribed, "Love is eternal." They were married in 1842. Afterward, Lincoln wrote a lawyer friend, "Nothing new here, except my marrying, which to me is a matter of wonder."

It was a wonder to many. Lincoln's law partner, William Herndon, despised Mary, referring to her as a "shrill" who made Abe's life miserable. She considered Herndon coarse, boozy, ill mannered, and antichurch.

As the wife of Congressman Lincoln, Mary grew bored and moved with the kids to her family's home in Kentucky. But she was overjoyed on November 6, 1860, when presidential candidate Lincoln told her, "Mary, we're elected."

Before the inauguration, Abe bought a silk hat and said, "Well, wife, if nothing else comes out of this, we are going to have some new clothes." She replied, "We are pleased with our advancement." At the inaugural ball, Mary danced a quadrille with Stephen Douglas, her husband's former opponent. She said the inauguration was the happiest night of her life.

Abe was right about the clothes. Mary loved splurging on shopping trips to New York and Philadelphia. She was criticized for wearing low-necked dresses and for the "flower beds on her head" (her flowery hats). Tending to plumpness and frumpiness in face and body, she tried to compensate with her garb. The amounts she spent on her personal wardrobe and White House furnishings provoked criticism.

And everyone noticed her touchiness. Some critics called her "Abe's Hellcat." One Northern lawyer referred to the Lincolns as "a smart country politician and a very vulgar old woman." Temperamental as Mary was, Abe was always extremely polite and fawning in her presence.

The Kentucky-born Mary was accused of being a Southern spy because her brother and three half-brothers were in the Rebel army. Confederate general Benjamin Hardin Helm was a brother-in-law of hers. The Senate's Committee on the Conduct of the War planned to investigate Mrs. Lincoln until Abe unexpectedly appeared before it and announced solemnly, "I, of my own knowledge, know that it is untrue that any of my family hold treasonable communication with the enemy."

MARY
TODD
LINCOLN

1818–1882

The shrew had her share of grief. After the death of their adored twelve-year-old son, Willie, in 1862, her behavior became erratic. She was so distraught that she did not attend Willie's funeral. Later, she was accused of visiting Mrs. Laury, a spiritualist, who was said to have told her about the condition of the deceased boy.

As the war ground on, Mary's disposition did not improve. While visiting City Point in Virginia, "Mrs. Lincoln repeatedly attacked her husband in the presence of officers," according to one observer, but Abe "bore it as Christ might have done, with supreme calmness and dignity; he called her 'Mother,' pleaded with eyes and tones, till she turned on him like a tigress, and then he walked away."

The first lady disliked Grant and said he was not fit for command. "I could lead an army as well myself," she claimed. On a steamboat on the Potomac, she said of Jefferson Davis, "Do not allow him to escape the law—he must be hanged!" Abe the Bible quoter replied, "'Judge not, that ye be not judged.'"

Not long before the assassination, she and Abe attended *The Marble Heart*, a play featuring John Wilkes Booth. Then Lincoln had an ominous dream forecasting his own death. She responded, "That is horrid! I wish you had not told it. I am glad I don't believe in dreams."

Lincoln did not particularly want to at-tend the second-rate play *Our American Cousin* at Ford's Theatre, but Mary had her heart set on it. She had cause to regret it. After Booth fired his fateful shot, Mary screamed and shouted, "He has shot the president!" Lincoln's head slumped forward, and Mary caught him to prevent his tumbling to the floor. She wailed, "My dear husband! My dear husband!" Mary was so distraught that she did not at-tend her husband's funeral.

She had a sizable inheritance, but her extravagance drove her into poverty. In 1870, Congress granted her a yearly pension of three thousand dollars (after she had indignantly petitioned Congress as the poor widow of a martyred president). Following the death of her youngest son, Tad, in 1871, she became more unstable and was committed to a private asylum for several months. Then, on May 19, 1875, a court declared her insane. That evening, she tried to commit suicide.

Afterward, she traveled abroad before returning to Springfield. Congress later increased her yearly pension to five thousand dollars and gave her a lump sum of fifteen thousand.

Abe's Hellcat, the wife of one of America's best-loved figures, is buried beside her husband and three of their children in Springfield, Illinois.

James Longstreet, Confederate General
(1821–1904)

OLD, SLOW WAR HORSE

WARS GIVE RISE to colorful nicknames. James Longstreet had two—"Old Pete," the name his soldiers called him, and "My Old War Horse," the affectionate name bestowed by his commander, Robert E. Lee. Critics have referred to him by other names, notably "Slowpoke" and "Peter the Slow." Looking at a picture of Longstreet's bland, somber face, it is a marvel that the man ever summoned the energy to crawl out of bed in the morning.

In fact, Old Pete was a fierce fighter—but not one who acted quickly. Whenever he disagreed with an order, he dragged his feet in acting on it. Inevitably, he crossed swords with Thomas "Stonewall" Jackson, who (since he prayed and stayed in constant communication with God) didn't like to be questioned. After Jackson was killed in 1863, Lee and Longstreet became chummier. Following Longstreet's good showing at the Battle of Antietam, Lee warmly embraced him and said, "Ah, here is Longstreet, here is my old war horse!" (Curiously, the War Horse was nursing a foot injury and had gone into battle wearing slippers made of carpet. Foot soldiers weren't the only Confederates in makeshift shoes in those years!)

Morale can be built in odd ways. The unflappable Longstreet gave his men confidence on more than one occasion by calmly puffing his cigar while bullets rained all around him. Like most officers in those days, he believed masculinity could be demonstrated by smoking cigars, drinking whiskey, playing poker, and jumping fences on one's horse.

Longstreet did have one quirk of attire that seems mildly feminine: he wore a gray shawl. Some took it as a sign of modesty, since it covered his insignia of rank.

Lee's Old War Horse had his share of burdens. During the war, scarlet fever killed three of his four children. After that blow, Longstreet became moodier and crankier. He also came close to suffering the same fate as Stonewall Jackson—death by friendly fire. After giving the Yankees what-for at the Battle of the Wilderness, Longstreet was wounded in the throat and arm by his own men and nearly bled to death. Lee desperately needed his general back in action, and Longstreet soon returned to the field despite a raspy voice and a paralyzed arm. On another occasion, he was wounded in the shoulder and apologized for weeping over his pain. An aide wrote to Longstreet's wife, "He says he does not see why a bullet going through a man's shoulder should make a baby of him."

Old Pete had an interesting Union connection. Before the war, he introduced a fellow West Point grad, Ulysses S. Grant, to his sweet but cross-eyed cousin, Julia Dent. The boozy Grant married the devout woman and had a satisfying marriage. During and after the war, Grant and Longstreet referred to each other as kinfolk. (Another West Point note: Longstreet's roommate there was William Rosecrans, who later became a noted Union general.)

Lee's Old War Horse actually hated war. Encamped near Petersburg, Virginia, he and Union general Edward Ord had an unofficial tête-à-tête and hatched a sensible plan for ending the bloodshed: Let the Union and Confederate generals suspend all fighting, and let the politicians hash out the details of a settlement. The idea (like all intelligent plans screwed up by politicians) went nowhere.

JAMES
LONGSTREET

1821–1904

The big blot on Old Pete's career was his slowness at the Battle of Gettysburg. Depending on how you look at it, Longstreet was a pessimist or a realist. Before the battle, he said, "I do not want to make this charge—I do not see how it can succeed." His delay in swinging his troops into action has been blamed for the South's loss.

Longstreet spent the rest of his life trying to lay the blame elsewhere. In his old age, he published *From Manassas to Appomattox*, probably one of the best Civil War memoirs. It should be taken with several grains of salt, though. Longstreet was not writing history but trying to gloss over his pathetic performance at Gettysburg. (Old soldiers never die, they just make excuses.) One reason the old man worked so hard to justify himself was that other Confederate generals—notably the foul-tempered Jubal Early—had united in a campaign to smear him. (Early called Longstreet a "viper" and a "renegade," among other things.)

They had a reason. After the war, Old Pete committed an unthinkable sin in the eyes of Southerners: he became a Republican. Horrors! The Republicans were the party of Abraham Lincoln, Ulysses S. Grant, abolitionists, damn Yankees, and various other damn things.

His other mortal sin: Longstreet venerated Robert E. Lee but dared to admit that Lee had some failings as a leader. After the war, and especially following his death in 1870, Lee became the Confederacy's saint, the valiant and flawless Christian gentleman. Longstreet was a realist, not an idealist, and hero worship was not in his nature. He dared to suggest that, yes, Lee was a great man, but . . . No former Confederates wanted to hear about the *but*. This won Longstreet no friends and made him quite a few enemies—an interesting turn of affairs, particularly since Lee and Longstreet had been close friends.

In his old age, Longstreet made pocket money by selling local produce at his Georgia home. The old soldier could have used a proofreader. The sign outside his home read, *"GOOD HOME MADE WINE SOLD CHEEP."*

George B. McClellan, Union General
(1826–1885)

LITTLE NAPOLEON BLUE

LIKE OTHER FAMOUS short men, Little Mac was determined to make a name for himself. He succeeded, though not always in a positive way.

McClellan was a boy wonder. He entered the University of Pennsylvania (its prep school, actually) a few months shy of age fourteen. When he was ready to enroll at West Point two years later, he was just under sixteen, the academy's minimum age. He was second in his class at West Point and gained fame in the Mexican War (a conflict that could rightly be called the "Rehearsal for the War Between the States").

At age thirty-four, Little Mac found himself in an enviable position. He was Lincoln's handpicked choice for commander of the Federal armies. The Union wasn't happy with the Confederates' triumph at First Manassas, and McClellan (so Lincoln thought) could turn things around.

McClellan repaid Lincoln's confidence with drilling, drilling, marching, marching, and more drilling. By the end of 1861, McClellan had whipped an army into shape, making thousands of green recruits look like real soldiers. Many of his men were proud to be part of what they called "McClellan's Army." He seemed to put the romance and adventure back into soldiering.

But it seemed he would never make his soldiers fight. Lincoln grew fidgety, particularly since McClellan refused to divulge what his military strategy was (if he had any). In January 1862, Lincoln issued his notorious General War Orders No. 1, announcing that as of February, the Union armies would attack the Confederates in Virginia. (A quote from Lincoln: "If the general is through marching the army around, I'd like to borrow it for awhile.")

The order didn't turn things around completely. Little Mac was loved by his troops for being a classy-looking military man, but he was noted for dawdling (which gained him another nickname, the "Virginia Creeper"). Lincoln accused him of having "the slows."

Historians suspect that if Mac had been more of a fighter than a drill instructor, the Union armies could have triumphed in 1862 instead of 1865—which would have made for a shorter war, less loss of life and property, and less time in healing the nation. Mac seemed so afraid of charging in half-cocked that he seldom charged in at all. He had the look but not the verve. Nonetheless, while on campaigns, he had his own portable printing press to distribute his grandiloquent messages to his men.

Little Mac always thought the enemy was stronger than it appeared. Rather stupidly, he always believed the vastly inflated reports of Confederate strength sent to him by the Union's spy chief, Allan Pinkerton. The Rebels used this to their advantage. On the Peninsula, the Confederates under General John Magruder (who was as pompous and vain as Mac) numbered only about 10,000. But Magruder used "Quaker guns" (logs painted to look like cannon) to fool Little Mac and his 105,000 men into thinking the Rebels numbered 100,000.

Mac's greatest military triumph was in fact a piece of dumb luck. A Union private found (wrapped around three cigars) the infamous "Lost Order," containing Robert E. Lee's plan for invading Maryland. Jubilant, Little Mac

GEORGE B.
McCLELLAN

1826–1885

responded by saying, "Here is a paper with which if I cannot whip Bobbie Lee I will be willing to go home." Well, he succeeded in one respect: Lee's army left Maryland in defeat. But McClellan's slowness and indecisiveness prompted Lincoln to remove him from command.

Like many ex-military men, McClellan dabbled in politics. He aimed for the top—the presidency—the goal being to run as a Democrat in 1864 and defeat his former commander, Lincoln. Dan Emmett, the Yankee who penned "Dixie," wrote Mac's campaign song, "Mac Will Win the Union Back." Mac didn't win. Apparently, Yankees thought the indecisive general would make an indecisive politician. And voters weren't convinced that Mac could make (as Democrats promised) an amicable peace with the South. Naturally, many Southerners prayed he would win.

The self-impressed little man who saw himself as Napoleon in blue did have some good qualities. Confederate general Robert Garnett was the first general killed in the war, and Mac graciously had his body returned to his family.

A couple of personal notes. One of Mac's battlefield opponents was Joe Johnston, a good friend before the war. They were such intimates that Johnston usually began his letters with "Beloved Mac." And McClellan had another connection with a Confederate general. His wife, Ellen Marcy, had turned down an earlier marriage proposal from A. P. Hill. (Ellen's family was appalled on finding out that Hill had gonorrhea—plus they liked Mac better anyway.)

George McClellan was one of America's greatest might-have-beens. He might have been the great Yankee Napoleon who defeated the Rebel forces. But that honor fell to two generals less prone to flaunting themselves, Ulysses S. Grant and William T. Sherman, both of whom knew how to fight. Which makes it all the more singular that the great Robert E. Lee, when asked after the war who was the ablest Federal general he had opposed, said without hesitation, "McClellan, by all odds." Sherman had a different assessment, stating to his wife that Little Mac "had too much staff, too many toadies, and looked too much to Number 1." And one of Lincoln's cabinet members had a short, to-the-point evaluation: "He liked show, parade, and power." Quite like Napoleon, except that Napoleon could fight.

George Gordon Meade, Union General
(1815–1872)

LINCOLN'S GREAT ALMOST

WAR IS MUCH MORE than charging, shooting, and killing. Fortifications and camps must be built, so someone has to understand the lay of the land. That was Meade's specialty. He never aspired to be supreme commander in the field and certainly never had the pride or vanity of a George McClellan or a John Pope. Like Ambrose Burnside, he stumbled into high command. It so happened that he stumbled into it during one of the great battles of history, Gettysburg.

Meade's portrait pretty much reveals the man's character. He looked (and was) well bred, dignified, genteel, definitely reserved, and capable of high temper on occasion. A fellow general called him a "simple, cold, serious soldier with his business-like air."

He went to West Point, but only after his doting mother concluded that the family couldn't afford a good private university. George had the face and build of an aristocrat but not the skills that should have gone with them. He chalked up numerous demerits at West Point because, like Sherman and Grant, he had no concern for spit and polish—the "show" side of military life that Winfield Scott and George McClellan cherished. But his fear of letting down Mama Meade led him to clean up his act.

In the Seminole Wars and in Mexico, he discovered his flair for engineering and surveying. Later, he worked on a massive government project on the Great Lakes, creating ship channels, dredging harbors, and building lighthouses. Dull-sounding stuff, but necessary nonetheless.

Meade was living in Michigan when the war began and was pro-Union, though he had some Southern ties. One sister was the mistress of a Mississippi plantation, and another had married into a prominent South Carolina clan. Meade refused to take part in a public oath-taking ceremony in which Federal officials pledged themselves to the Union. It looked like he was washed up where Federal jobs were concerned, but his wife pulled some strings to get him appointed an officer under McClellan.

Meade fought in the Peninsula campaign in Virginia and was wounded at White Oak Swamp. He half-ignored what he thought was a trivial wound until he noticed his saddle was drenched with blood. Meade had been shot (in the back, as it turned out) by a Rebel sharpshooter. Nonetheless, he continued to direct the battle until he nearly collapsed. At another battle, two bullets passed through his hat and one through his horse's neck. The man was hard to frighten.

Like everyone else, Meade grew frustrated at Little Mac's slowness. "McClellan's vice," Meade wrote, "was always waiting to have everything just as he wanted before he would attack, and before he could get things arranged as he wanted them, the enemy pounced on him and thwarted all his plans." Meade was equally unimpressed (as was Lincoln) with Burnside and Hooker, Mac's lackluster successors at the head of the Army of the Potomac.

After Hooker's smashing defeat at Chancellorsville, Lincoln's generals wondered who would be next to inherit the "commander's curse." Was Meade the one? He was certainly brave enough. Whoever

GEORGE
GORDON
MEADE

1815–1872

it turned out to be would have to deal with a jarring reality: Lee and his army had invaded Pennsylvania.

At three o'clock one morning, a courier awoke Meade with a request: Would he accept command of the Army of the Potomac? Meade raised several objections, but the courier made it clear that Lincoln himself had picked his man. Meade replied, "I've been tried and condemned without a hearing, and I suppose I shall have to go to execution." He and his son, also named George, went to break the news to Joe Hooker, who was not surprised. To Meade's dismay, Hooker knew practically nothing about Lee's movements. The new commander got little prepping.

Some Billy Yanks asked, "What has Meade ever done?" He was brave and reliable, true, but the soldiers were used to McClellan's and Hooker's boasting and swagger, so Meade seemed a little, well, uninspiring. Meade was aware that some called him a "damned old goggle-eyed snapping turtle." But Robert E. Lee was on Yankee soil, and the goggle-eyed turtle set out to greet him and defeat him.

Three days after his appointment as commander, Meade found out where Lee was: near Gettysburg. There, from July 1 to July 3, 1863, Meade managed his troops well. Since the historic battle was a Union victory (though with staggering losses on both sides), Meade received the official Thanks of Congress. Under his leadership, the Army of the Potomac sent the Army of Northern Virginia back home, with no incentive to return.

There was plenty of finger pointing (then and later) among the Confederates. Abe Lincoln was also disappointed, as usual. Why, he lamented, had Meade not pursued the beaten Johnny Rebs and annihilated them? The Potomac River was swollen, which delayed Lee's crossing. Alas, a golden opportunity was lost, or so Lincoln believed. (In fairness to Meade, Lincoln misread the situation and seriously overestimated how vulnerable Lee was at that time. Meade was being wise and cautious, and Lincoln had come to detest caution in his generals.)

For the remainder of the war, Meade was eclipsed by the rising sun of Grant, who had Meade's modesty and bravery plus a darn sight more aggression. Lincoln had found his man.

At Appomattox, after Lee's surrender to Grant, Meade dropped in to pay his respects to Lee. A few days later in Richmond, he did the same. The two had been friends before the war, and both were gentlemen. Lee made some remark about the gray in Meade's beard, and Meade replied, "*You* are responsible for my gray hairs."

Old soldiers do die. Meade died in Philadelphia in 1872, his old war wounds combining forces with pneumonia to take the general to his grave. He died before the "battle of the books," the flood of memoirs by former generals praising themselves and blaming others.

But Meade had registered his opinion before his death: "I don't believe the truth will ever be known, and I have a great contempt for history."

John S. Mosby, Confederate Partisan Leader
(1833–1916)

RED-HEADED GHOST ON HORSEBACK

FEW CIVIL WAR figures have been the hero of a popular TV series. Cavalry officer Mosby was. Beginning in 1957, *The Gray Ghost* featured actor Tod Andrews as Major John Mosby. The show was nothing more than a Confederate horse opera, but its very existence says something about Mosby's appeal. How many Civil War of-

ficers besides the generals are known today? Very few. Mosby, who at his zenith was a colonel, was and still is the best-known non-general.

The little redhead known as the "Gray Ghost" was a lawyer by trade. He came into the law by running afoul of it. While at the University of Virginia, he shot a fellow student and was sent to prison. He made good use of his prison time studying law and was admitted to the bar after his release.

But the gritty redhead liked to ride, so when war came, he joined the cavalry and fought at First Manassas. He was a scout for Jeb Stuart and the source of the idea for Stuart's famous "Ride around McClellan."

Having an independent streak, Mosby became a leader of partisan rangers (military units used for the purpose of making inroads into enemy territory). These "approved guerrillas" were accountable to the Confederate military but semi-independent.

Mosby's Rangers were the most famous of the partisan bands. The northern Virginia counties of Fauquier and Loudoun, his home base, were known as "Mosby's Confederacy." His stated purpose was "to weaken the armies invading Virginia by harassing their rear." But he did more than that.

Mosby's elite, highly mobile band was the source of some colorful tales. On a rainy night in March 1863, he and twenty-nine men stole into Fairfax Courthouse, Virginia, and the camp of Union general Edwin Stoughton—who was in bed with a floozy. The Gray Ghost awakened Stoughton with a swat on his bare behind and asked if he had ever heard of Mosby. The shocked general replied, "Yes! Tell me, have you caught the rascal?" "No," said the chuckling Mosby, "but he has caught you!"

Such tales of daring delighted the South and infuriated the North. Grant ordered that if Mosby or any of his rangers were captured, they were to be hanged without trial. On one occasion, Lincoln pardoned one of Mosby's Rangers when the man's tearful wife begged for mercy. General George Armstrong Custer was not so kind. He executed six of the rangers, along with a seventeen-year-old boy who had run away to join Mosby; Custer's men shot him as his widowed mother begged for mercy. The Yanks tied a placard around one of the suspended bodies. It read, "This will be the fate of Mosby and all his men." It wasn't.

Like the picturesque Stuart, the Gray Ghost was a romantic figure. Like Stuart, he wore a plume in his hat and a cape of red silk. A newspaper report described him thus: "His figure is slight, muscular, supple, and vigorous; his eye is keen, penetrating, ever on the alert; he wears his saber and pistol with the air of a man who sleeps with them. . . . The major is a determined man in a charge, dangerous on a scout, hard to outwit, and prone to turn up suddenly where he is least expected, and bang away with pistol and carbine." (The saber might have been just a prop for the reporter; Mosby, a practical man, preferred an

JOHN S.
MOSBY

1833–1916

extra pistol to a cumbersome saber.) Confederate civilians devoured such accounts, and Virginians gladly concealed and fed the ever-roving rangers.

Mosby traveled light. At their peak, his rangers numbered about eight hundred men, who were organized in bands of from twenty to eighty and were able to disperse and regroup quickly when necessary. On one occasion, they seized a railroad train and $178,000 in Union greenbacks (a valuable haul, considering how worthless Confederate money had become). Mosby despised the Confederate military bureaucracy. "Although a revolutionary government, none was ever so much under the domination of red tape as Richmond," he wrote. So he enjoyed his footloose partisan role, detached from official orders spewed out by telegraph.

Regular Confederate soldiers envied the partisan rangers, calling them "feather-bed soldiers" and "spoiled darlings" for the freedom they had. In fact, it took a special breed of man to make a successful (and living) partisan. Yes, they appeared wild, free, and romantic. But their casualty rate was high—around 40 percent. And behind the partisan life was a serious purpose: keeping the Union armies harassed, occupied, and observed. Call them scouts or spies, the partisans were indispensable as "eyes" for the Confederacy. Mosby pro-

vided Lee with valuable information—so much so that he was mentioned in more of Lee's official reports than any other officer.

After hearing of Joseph Johnston's surrender to Sherman in North Carolina, Mosby wisely disbanded his rangers, so neither he nor they ever surrendered to the Federals. The spunky man then went back to the practice of law (which must have been a dramatic change from his wild days on horseback).

Shortly before Robert E. Lee died, he ran into Mosby in Richmond. Mosby arranged a meeting among himself, Lee, and George Pickett, who still blamed Lee for the massacre of his division at Gettysburg. The uncomfortable meeting was not a success.

Mosby lived to a ripe old age. At his retirement, he was serving in the Department of Justice under Theodore Roosevelt. By that time, he was a one-eyed widower known as a cantankerous character with memories of a wild youth. Mosby's colorful memoirs, published after his death, are probably one of the most-read accounts by a key actor in the Civil War. They end with the rather bittersweet statement, "No one clung longer to the Confederacy than I did."

Legend has it that it was Mosby who coined the political term *Solid South*, which referred to the solidly Democratic (until the 1980s, that is) bloc of Southern states.

George Pickett, Confederate General
(1825–1875)

FIRST IN HIS CLASS

IN HIS 1846 West Point class, Pickett ranked first—first from the bottom, that is. Perhaps primping leaves little time for academics. Pickett was a notoriously pretty man who curled both his hair and beard in ringlets and wore so much cologne that another general claimed, "The Yanks will smell the breeze and swear they're close to a whorehouse or Pickett." But he also showed that he truly wanted to be part of the Confederate army. When the war broke out, he left his United States Army post in the Pacific Northwest and sailed all the way around South America to reach Virginia.

Pretty Pickett's Civil War claim to fame

is that he led an ill-fated charge at the ill-fated Battle of Gettysburg. If not for that disaster, it's doubtful that his name would have made it to the history books. People still puzzle that almost his entire division became casualties in the span of less than an hour, while Pickett himself emerged without a scratch. (Was he somewhere having his beard curled?) After Gettysburg, he said, "All the glory in the world could never atone for the widows and orphans this day has made."

Post-Gettysburg, Pickett coped with his humiliation in a sensible fashion: he took a furlough and married a woman half his age. At the time, he had been a widower for twelve years. His new bride was the romantically named Miss LaSalle Corbell of Chuckatuck. Pickett's fellow generals believed that his courting of LaSalle distracted him from his duties. More than once, he took an unofficial leave to pay his respects to his lady fair. (In fact, he had dashed off a note to her just seconds before his Gettysburg charge.)

Pickett also suffered a blow after Gettysburg: his ancestral home on Turkey Island in the James River was burned to the ground. To add insult to injury, the Union general behind the burning was the cross-eyed and mostly incompetent Benjamin Butler, the "Beast of New Orleans." Pickett then enjoyed a minor consolation when his army successfully bottled up Butler's forces for a time.

There was one bright spot through it all: LaSalle gave Pickett a healthy baby boy. Pickett's old buddy, a Union man named Ulysses S. Grant, sent him a gift across the battle lines: a silver service for the newborn.

Not long afterward, Lee ordered Pickett to hold an important junction. While Pickett was chowing down at a shad bake, his entire division was destroyed by the Yanks at Five Forks. (Pickett tried to compensate for his late arrival by waving a bloody Rebel flag and singing "Rally 'Round the Flag, Boys.") One day before the Appomattox surrender, Lee dismissed his controversial general.

That wasn't the final blow. When the war was done, infamy was heaped on Pickett for simply doing his duty. Confederate law said that Southern men who joined the Union army were to be executed by hanging. These were the Civil War's Tories, and loyal Confederates despised them. Pickett had executed twenty-two such men in Kinston, North Carolina, only to find that the Federals were ready to prosecute him for war crimes after the conflict. He hightailed it to Canada, a favorite destination for ex-Rebels fearing retribution. His old buddy Grant pleaded for mercy on Pickett's behalf. President Andrew Johnson

GEORGE
PICKETT

1825–1875

heeded Grant's plea and granted clemency to the relieved Pickett.

After the war, Pickett met only once with Robert E. Lee, his commanding general at Gettysburg. The meeting was decidedly uncomfortable. Once outside the room where they talked, Pickett bitterly exclaimed, "That old man had my division massacred." Pickett was definitely *not* part of the growing legion of Southerners who made Lee into their Confederate saint.

What does a humiliated soldier with a bad reputation do after a war? Pickett sold life insurance. After his death at age fifty, his widow, LaSalle, published *Pickett and His Men*, which (to no one's surprise) made her husband out to be a hero.

One little oddity worth noting: Richmond, capital of the Confederacy, keeper of the flame of the "Lost Cause," was the birthplace of only one famous Confederate general, and that was Pickett. No doubt, some Richmond residents feel a twinge of shame that their most famous local boy was a failure (now that we can look back objectively) and someone whose military career was undeserving of all the attention it has received. Just the same, Pickett was buried in one of the great resting places of the Confederate dead, Richmond's famous Hollywood Cemetery.

John Pope, Union General
(1822–1892)

LITTLE MAC'S VEXATIOUS STAND-IN

HOW COULD ONE MAN vex so many people? No ordinary man could. It took a vainglorious egotist with an overactive tongue. That was the lot of John Pope, who might hold title to the Union army's supreme ego (though he had some serious competition).

He always liked attention. In his West Point days, he did something shocking: he wore pants that (gasp!) buttoned on the front instead of the side. The academy's superintendent liked the innovation and made it standard. But it raised eyebrows at the time, maybe because the opening was in, well, the obvious place. How times change.

One fellow general stated, "I don't care for John Pope one pinch of owl dung."

Some generals thought even less. One of Lincoln's cabinet members told the president, "Old John Pope, his father, was a flatterer, a deceiver, a liar, and a trickster, and all the Popes are so."

Yet the Union faced a problem. Who could lead the Northern armies to victory in Virginia, when the South had such luminaries as Lee and Jackson? George McClellan, a small man with a humongous ego, boasted he could do the job but failed. In the days before Grant and Sherman began to shine, Lincoln was vexed and perplexed. Who was the Union's man of the hour? Who could conquer Virginia?

Enter John Pope. He had been one of Lincoln's military escorts en route to his presidential inauguration. His father was a judge Lincoln knew in Illinois. And soldiering was Pope's lifework. He was a former Mexican War officer who had been promoted for gallantry. He was also an explorer and a true-blue 1860 Republican. His Civil War victories included taking six thousand prisoners at Island No. 10 on the Mississippi. That victory came against vastly inferior and poorly led defenses, but it made Pope's reputation anyway.

Pope already had another reputation—as a bad handler of men. For example, early in the war, a New York captain had deserted his command, and Pope had shown his contempt by posting a reward of five cents for the man's capture. Still, Lincoln made him commander of the new Army of Virginia, moving the sluggish McClellan elsewhere. John C. Frémont, American hero and the West's famous "Pathfinder," resigned from the army rather than serve under Pope. (Considering what an embarrassment the Pathfinder was as a general, this might have been the most positive thing to come of Pope's command.) McClellan wrote his wife, "I don't see how I can remain in the service if placed under Pope, it would be too great a disgrace." McClellan had no desire to see Pope succeed where he himself had failed. He licked his lips, hoping Pope would suffer defeat and humiliation.

Well liked or not, Pope had his mission, and he took it seriously. To his new command, the Army of Virginia, he bragged, "I have come to you from the West, where we have always seen the back of our enemies." This rankled many of the Eastern soldiers. (Confederate general Ewell responded, "By God, he'll never see the backs of my men. Their pants are out at the rear, and the sight would paralyze this western bully.") Pope predicted that "success and glory are in the advance, disaster and shame lurk in the rear." He didn't foresee the disaster and shame lurking ahead.

Encamped in Virginia, he wrote his letters from what he called his "Headquarters in the Saddle." (Lincoln joked that the general

JOHN
POPE

1822–1892

had his "headquarters where his hindquarters ought to be.") Pope also published a series of Draconian rules governing the conduct of civilians in his path—rules threatening wholesale imprisonments as well as executions. One example: If any Union soldier was fired upon from a house, the house would be razed and the inhabitants sent to military prisons. There was no precedent for this vile treatment of civilians, but mostly it was typical Pope bluster, as few actual punishments were meted out. Nonetheless, the order provoked the Virginia-loving Robert E. Lee to inform his generals that Pope had to be "suppressed."

Pope suffered a curious humiliation at the hands of Confederate cavalry wizard Jeb Stuart. On August 22, 1862, Stuart raided Pope's camp, capturing $350,000 in Union currency, Pope's coat and hat, and several members of his staff, along with information on Union movements. Stuart gleefully presented the coat to Stonewall Jackson: "General! I've got Pope's coat! If you don't believe it, there's his name!" The somber Jackson saluted and replied, "General Stuart, I would much rather you had brought General Pope instead of his coat." (Stuart thus got even for earlier losing his famous red-lined cloak to Pope's men.)

Then came August 29 and 30, 1862. Second Manassas in northern Virginia was the test. Was Pope all bluster or a real fighter? Answer: bluster. He lost fourteen thousand out of eighty thousand men, while Lee lost nine thousand out of fifty-four thousand. A wounded and dying colonel of the First Michigan Cavalry wrote to his family, "I am one of the victims of Pope's imbecility." As the defeated Union army straggled back toward Washington, people began to vamoose, fearing a Confederate invasion. Outbound trains were packed. The South was elated, the North mortified.

Pope was relieved of command and assigned to the Northwest to curb the Indians. Yet the president spoke favorably of him and believed he had not had a fair chance. "Pope did well," Lincoln said, "but there was an army prejudice against him, and it was necessary he should leave." He said of Second Manassas, "We had the enemy in the hollow of our hands on Friday, if our generals, who are vexed with Pope, had done their duty. All of our present difficulties and reverses have been brought upon us by these quarrels of the generals." Lincoln was sure that McClellan and his clique had schemed to "break down Pope."

What McClellan and his fan club hoped and (no doubt) prayed for came to pass: Pope failed, and Lincoln recalled Little Mac. It was a case of a new loser replaced by an old loser.

William Clarke Quantrill, Confederate Guerrilla
(1 8 3 7 – 1 8 6 5)

<u>BAD TO THE BONE</u>

SOME BAD MEN are bad from the word *go*. Quantrill was. Like many killers, his first experiences in cruelty were with animals. As a child, he nailed snakes to trees and watched them squirm. He shot pigs through the ears to hear them squeal. He tied two cats' tails together and threw them over a clothesline, then laughed as they clawed each other to death. While walking through farmers' fields, he stabbed horses and cattle just for fun. He was cruel to humans, too. He locked a girl in a church belfry and threw away the key. He carried snakes in his pockets and tossed them at little girls.

This sadist from Ohio who identified

with the Confederacy was one of the Civil War's nastier personalities. In fact, the rogue had no loyalty at all; all evidence suggests he hated the whole human race. But war gives dishonest and bloodthirsty men a chance to make an easy living, often in the name of patriotism.

Before the war, Quantrill was already a criminal. His outlaw alias was Charley Hart. He stole horses and cattle, then "tracked them down" to collect rewards from the owners. In Missouri, he stole slaves, then resold them to their owners for the reward money. Across the border in Kansas, he kidnapped free blacks and sold them into slavery in Missouri. When he wasn't stealing slaves or livestock, Charley Hart gambled, drank, wrestled, and lolled around with women of easy virtue.

When war came, Quantrill knew he could not stand taking orders or drilling in a regular military unit. But he liked the idea of killing and being applauded for it. He had lived in the Indian territory and learned guerrilla tactics from the Cherokees. So, based in Missouri, he assembled a gang of cutthroats who had no love for either the Confederacy or the Union but who identified themselves (purely for convenience) as Confederates. Their purpose: vex the Union army and pro-Union civilians in any way possible, including killing them, burning bridges, cutting telegraph lines, whatever. A favorite tactic: Quantrill's men would dress in Union blue, amble up pleasantly to a Federal unit, then open fire at point-blank range. Dirty, but effective.

Western Missouri came to be called "Quantrill Country." Most of Quantrill's men, being locals, were familiar with the back roads and hidden paths. Pro-Confederate residents of Quantrill Country were glad to shelter the raiders, who were much better fed and clothed than most Confederate soldiers. And no one denied that Quantrill's men were among the best shots in any army, North or South.

Some of his gang members were famous in their own right: Jesse and Frank James and the Younger brothers, Cole, Jim, and Bob. Then there was Bloody Bill Anderson, who tied a knot in a silken cord for every man he killed. (Final tally: fifty-four.) He may have actually been more heartless than Quantrill, though it was a close race. Quantrill would give a sadistic giggle (a "gay, nervous chuckle," as one observer described it) right after he killed a man. Anderson, they said, foamed at the mouth while in the heat of killing.

Quantrill operated outside the system, but like most renegades, he still craved the approval of the authorities. In August 1862, he and his men were officially mustered into the

WILLIAM
CLARKE
QUANTRILL

1837–1865

Confederate army as a partisan ranger company. Quantrill was made a captain. He was extremely proud of being "official" and carried his commission with him. He resented the regular Confederate troops in his area for their rules and their habit of *not* murdering prisoners of war.

In late 1862, he went to Richmond, hoping to be the toast of the town and meet with President Davis. No dice. Confederate authorities were scandalized by the bushwhackers' tactics. Quantrill did meet with Secretary of War James Seddon, who did not give him the colonel's commission he desired. But afterward, Quantrill claimed Seddon had—and he called himself "colonel."

Quantrill is remembered for a notorious massacre of civilians in Lawrence, Kansas, in August 1863. Kansas was in fact a bloody place before Quantrill arrived. Proslavery "bushwhackers" and antislavery "jayhawkers" had been slaughtering each other (and innocent bystanders) for years. Lawrence was notoriously antislavery, so it was a natural target for Quantrill's men.

Quantrill planned the Lawrence raid carefully. His guiding order: "Kill every man big enough to carry a gun." There were about 450 men in his band of raiders. They rode full tilt into town at daybreak, hollering the Rebel yell and firing pistols. The mayor, who was high on Quantrill's death list, hid in his well. Quantrill's raiders burned his house, including the wellhouse; he suffocated inside the well. During the raid, Quantrill calmly ate a hearty breakfast at the City Hotel.

The final tally in Lawrence: 185 men and boys dead, many of them burned. Left behind were 85 widows and 250 fatherless children. More than a hundred houses were destroyed, as were seventy-five buildings in the business district. One notable building was untouched: the armory, with its weapons neatly stacked inside. Stupidly, the mayor of the notoriously pro-Union town had mandated that no one could be armed within the city limits, which made Quantrill's work much easier.

"Colonel" Quantrill lay low for a while. Eventually, he decided to move his cutthroat gang to Kentucky. He even hatched a plan to assassinate Lincoln, though John Wilkes Booth beat him to it.

Quantrill had a premonition of his own death when his horse, Old Charley, was injured and had to be shot. Quantrill turned deathly pale and said, "That means my work is done. Death is coming."

Hiding out on a farm, Quantrill was asleep in a hayloft when Union men surrounded the barn. He was shot in the spine. He lingered for nearly a month in a military prison hospital. Nursed by a Catholic priest, he was baptized as a Catholic at the end. Quantrill gave the priest four thousand dollars, asking him to spend half on a headstone and give the other half to his wife, Kate. Rumor has it that Kate (whom Quantrill married when she was fourteen) used her portion of the money to start a highly successful whorehouse.

Quantrill's boys began holding reunions in 1889, with Cole Younger as the centerpiece. The men convened near Independence, Missouri, and always displayed a large, framed painting of Quantrill prominently. The passing of time turned the cutthroats into Confederate Robin Hoods, good Southern heroes. But many years after the war, Frank James said, "The truth was, we were nothing but great big boys." He could have said, more accurately, "We were nothing but sadistic sociopaths."

The last reunion was held in 1929.

William S. Rosecrans, Union General
(1819–1898)

THE ROSE OF CHICKAMAUGA

WITH A NAME like Rosecrans, a nickname is inevitable. To both Union and Confederate soldiers, the general was always "Old Rosey" or just "Rosey." Like his fellow Union general Burnside, Rosey was a nice guy. One officer described him thus: "A fine, hearty, abrupt sort of talker, heavy-whiskered . . . keen eyes, with light brows and lashes, head shunted forward a little, legs a little unsteady in walk . . . chatty and sociable." He had what one observer called "an intensified Roman nose." Blond himself, he said he preferred "sandy fellows" because they were "quick and sharp," and more industrious than brunettes. Also like Burnside, he was an overall failure as a general. Though fellow officers called him "that wily Dutchman," he wasn't wily enough to make a good commander.

Rosey was an Ohio boy. If Virginia was the great breeding ground for Confederate generals, Ohio served that purpose for the Union. Among the Union notables from Ohio were Grant, Sherman, and Sheridan, to name just a few.

But Rosey was a rarity in the top ranks of either army: a Catholic. He became one while a cadet at West Point, to the great dismay of his devout Protestant parents. (His brother also became a Catholic—and bishop of Cincinnati to boot!) Rosey carried both a cross and a rosary in his pocket. He would keep his staff up until four in the morning discussing spiritual matters. He was described as pious but could let loose a torrent of profanity on occasion—though he claimed he never took the name of God in vain. (He drew a sharp distinction between profanity and blasphemy. On one occasion he scolded foul-mouthed General Philip Sheridan by saying, "Watch your language! Remember the first bullet may send you to eternity!") He saw no reason to be a teetotaler and was a noted consumer of whiskey, which no doubt made his red face even redder.

The West Point grad taught engineering for four years at the academy before going on to success as an engineer and oil prospector. Before Stonewall Jackson was given his teaching post at the Virginia Military Institute, the school considered Rosecrans.

When war came, Rosey chalked up some victories in Mississippi and was made commander of the Army of the Cumberland. True to its name, that army operated mostly in Tennessee. At Murfreesboro, Rosecrans and Confederate general Braxton Bragg launched simultaneous assaults on the morning of January 2, 1863. Rosecrans occupied the town afterward. Technically, he had won, but his army was so worn down that it lay inert for six months. Following Murfreesboro, there was a wave of "absenteeism" (men sick, or pretending to be). In one typical brigade, there were sixteen hundred men present and thirteen hundred absent.

But levity sometimes snuck in. On one occasion, Rosey rode by several soldiers down on all fours, barking like dogs. That was the common reaction against the army's new two-man tents, a widely disliked downsizing from the old six-man tents. The men called the new models "dog tents" or "dog pens," but "pup tents" eventually became the standard name. Some men hung signs on their tents with such messages as PUPS FOR SALE, DOGHOLE NO. 1, and even SONS OF BITCHES WITHIN.

WILLIAM S.
ROSECRANS

1819–1898

After the call for lights out, the general would walk among the tents. When he spotted a light burning, he would whack the side of the tent with his sword (the flat side, of course). It was a curious mixture of discipline and play, and the men seemed to like it.

The Battle of Chickamauga, fought near the Georgia-Tennessee line on September 19 and 20, 1863, was Rosey's undoing. He faced Braxton Bragg again, only this time, Bragg clearly won. Rosecrans and two other generals were charged with misconduct. (Rumor was that he was being sacked for "opium-eating, fits of religious melancholy, and gross personal misconduct.") All three generals were acquitted, but Rosey was nonetheless replaced by George Thomas, the "Rock of Chickamauga," who had saved Rosecrans's army from complete destruction. Lincoln claimed that Rosecrans had acted "confused and stunned like a duck hit on the head." It fulfilled the prophecy of Secretary of War Stanton, who had never wanted Rosey to command the Army of the Cumberland. Stanton had said to Lincoln, "You have made your choice of idiots. Now you can expect the news of a terrible disaster!"

In 1864, Rosey claimed he had unearthed a plot in which the Order of American Knights, a pro-Southern underground group, would assassinate Lincoln and take over the government. He estimated that the American Knights numbered more than 150,000 members in Missouri, Illinois, Ohio, and Indiana. They were supposedly planning a kind of civil war in the North. Paranoia ran high during the war, but eventually the "conspiracy" was shrugged off. The Union had enough *real* opponents to deal with.

The Union army apparently never forgave Rosey for Chickamauga. After 1864, he was never given a command. He resigned from the army in 1867, not that anyone minded.

After the war, Andrew Johnson appointed him minister to Mexico. Grant removed him from that post the following year, and Rosey retired to his ranch in California. In 1880, his former chief of staff in the Army of the Cumberland, James Garfield, was elected president. Rosey died in 1898.

Edmund Ruffin, Secessionist
(1794–1865)

A SHOT OF GRAY EMINENCE

WHEN THE CONFEDERACY died, so did Ruffin. He shot himself. His children told his grandchildren, "The Yankees killed your grandfather." In a way, it was true. Ruffin had devoted much of his long life to getting the Southern states to secede from the Union, only to watch his work collapse with the Confederacy's surrender in 1865. When the Yankees beat the South, Ruffin had no reason to live. He gave much thought to his suicide, even searching the Bible to determine if self-murder was truly murder in God's eyes. He concluded it wasn't and shot himself through the head. It was the second fateful shot of his life, the other being the shot at Fort Sumter that kicked off the Civil War.

Who was this silver-haired patriarch of secession? He began life as a Virginia Tidewater plantation lad, his family rooted in the Old Dominion since 1666. Intelligent and well read, Edmund was one planter who took a genuine interest in the welfare of his lands and even, yes, his slaves. Ruffin was one of the few people in the 1800s to approach farming scientifically. He saw that tobacco farming was wearing out Virginia's soil. After reading everything he could get his hands on, he concluded that a substance called *marl* was the best way to rejuvenate his lands. Neighbors scoffed until his much-increased harvests proved he was no fool. He published essays and books on his methods; he met a lot of resistance but made some converts, too. By the 1840s, most Tidewater farmers had adopted his methods. He gave one of his prosperous plantations the appropriate name Marlbourne.

Ruffin might have gone down in history as an agricultural reformer had he restricted his publishing efforts to farming. But like most men of celebrity in those days, he felt compelled to take a stand politically. To no one's surprise, the successful plantation master took a states' rights, pro-South, anti-abolition stand. Curiously, in that same period, he petitioned Virginia's governor to pardon a slave who had been accused (wrongly, in Ruffin's view) of

murder and sentenced to death. Ruffin was a rarity in that he did not hire white overseers for his slaves but gave the reins to a trusted slave, Jem Sykes, who had the keys to every building on his plantation.

But mostly, Ruffin devoted his energy to his magazines, the *Southern Review* among them. Under the pen name "A Virginian," he also contributed some widely read pro-secession articles to newspapers in Richmond and Charleston. When he was made Virginia's agricultural commissioner, he used his bully pulpit to address audiences not only on farming but (surprise!) on politics.

Some nation-shaking events made Ruffin want to do more than lecture. When John Brown was captured at Harpers Ferry in 1859, Ruffin rushed to the scene, hoping a war would begin when abolitionists came to rescue Brown. Ruffin arrived to find himself a Southern celebrity. To the delight of many (and probably the giggles of others), the old man joined a company of Virginia Military Institute cadets on guard at Brown's hanging. It was a win-win situation: the abolitionists would precipitate a war if they showed up to rescue Brown, or the villain Brown would be hanged. Brown was hanged. Later, Ruffin embarked on a speaking tour in which he showed audiences the fearsome-looking pikes that John Brown's "army" had intended to use on slave owners.

EDMUND
RUFFIN

1794–1865

He sent Brown's pikes to every Southern governor. His message was clear: these abolitionists were bloodthirsty fanatics, and the sooner the South was out of the Union, the better.

Seeing war on the horizon, Ruffin put his writing talents to work in *Anticipations of the Future*, a novel depicting the events he believed would follow Southern secession. Back in the real world, he was gleeful when Lincoln was elected president. He hastened to South Carolina, eager to do whatever was needed (and not much was) to push it to secede. When it did, Ruffin was overjoyed. Upon the formation of the Confederacy, he announced he would not return to Virginia until it joined the new C.S.A. He became the toast of Charleston.

Ruffin (so the story goes) fired the first shot at Fort Sumter. Truth or legend? He was definitely on the scene, having joined the much younger men of the Palmetto Guards. The commander of the Confederate forces selected the Palmetto Guards to fire the first shots before dawn on April 12, 1861, and they (or so we are told) gave Mr. Secession the honor. The shell he fired struck Sumter, and the Civil War began. Soon afterward, he had another honor: one of his sons named his newborn baby Edmund Sumter Ruffin. Even better was the news that Virginia had indeed seceded.

Back home in the Old Dominion, Ruffin was present at the first major Confederate victory, First Manassas, where he fired a cannon at some retreating Yankees. He later learned to his pleasure that at least six were killed.

But it was nothing but bad news from then on. He and his large clan were forced to flee when the Yankees invaded their home turf. The invaders, well aware that the property belonged to the patriarch of secession, wrote on the walls (in charcoal and tobacco juice) such messages as THIS HOUSE BELONGED TO A RUFFINLY SON OF A BITCH and IT IS A PITY YOU GO UNHANGED. Perhaps even more painful, the man who had been so kind to his slaves found that they had flown the coop anyway. No doubt that amused the abolitionists.

Ruffin had donated much of his money to the Confederate treasury. His writings and speeches had helped bring secession about. He had literally lit the spark that ignited the war. Now, the Yankees had wreaked havoc with his lifework. The Confederacy had surrendered, and Lincoln had been assassinated, ensuring that the South faced nothing but vengeance from the North. Ruffin was already seventy-one years old and no doubt very tired.

His last diary entry, on June 17, 1865, made it clear why he was exiting the world: "I here declare my unmitigated hatred to Yankee rule . . . and to the Yankee race."

Winfield Scott, Union General
(1786–1866)

MOUNTAIN-SIZE MILITARY MENTOR

IF MILITARY SUCCESS is measured by the amount of land taken, Mexican War leader Scott was a biggie. Texas, Arizona, Nevada, California, Utah, parts of New Mexico, Colorado, and Wyoming—1,193,000 square miles, an area five times the size of France, Europe's largest nation.

The great general was a biggie in al-most every sense. He was six-foot-five and, at his peak, about three hundred pounds. He liked the showy side of military life and wore lots of gold braid, huge epaulettes on his shoulders, and a plumed hat. "Old Fuss and Feathers" was a sight.

Scott's long life is almost a capsule his-tory of American wars of the 1800s. He was involved in every war, big and small, from the War of 1812 through the Civil War. His enormous body had several bullets lodged in it—painful souvenirs of the wars. Even after his retirement, his influence lingered in the dozens of Civil War leaders he had impressed in his younger days.

He took drilling and regulations seriously but kept his officers happy with nightly socials. These were not just chat sessions, but events at which future luminaries like Robert E. Lee received much of their military education from the vain but wise old Scott. The young Thomas J. Jackson (before he became "Stonewall") wrote that Scott was "by far the most talented and scientific, and at the same time the most vain and conceited general." Scott was also generous with his praise of subordinates, including Jackson himself.

America has a long tradition of turning its victorious generals into presidents. Look at George Washington, Andrew Jackson, Zachary Taylor, U. S. Grant, and Dwight Eisenhower. The formidable Scott almost made the list. He was the Whig Party's presidential candidate in 1852 and won 44 percent of the popular vote. Yet he lost out to another Mexican War veteran, the slimmer, handsomer Franklin Pierce, who proved to be a rather colorless and lackluster commander in chief.

But Scott was not forgotten. He became, to no one's surprise, the head of all United States troops.

When the Civil War began, Scott was seventy-five. His massive body was swollen with dropsy, partly due to his fondness for good food (lots of it) and wine (lots of that, too). His favorite dish was Maryland terrapin, which he called "the finest food vouchsafed by God to man." By then, he could not mount his horse but had to be hoisted into the saddle. He spent most of his days lying on his office sofa.

Scott had been born in Virginia, but he had no intention of joining up with the Confederacy. Years earlier, he had had some experience with secession; in 1833, President Andrew Jackson had sent him with troops to Charleston when South Carolina threatened to secede. Now it was 1861, and secession was a reality.

The newly elected Lincoln sent a messenger to Scott to find out how loyal the Virginia man-mountain was. Propped up on pillows in his bed, the fleshy old man wheezed out, "Say to him that, when once here, I shall consider myself responsible for his safety. If necessary I'll plant cannon at both ends of Pennsylvania Avenue, and if any even venture to raise a finger, I'll blow them to hell." In fact, on the day of Lincoln's inauguration, Scott

WINFIELD
SCOTT

1786–1866

ordered crack riflemen placed on the roofs of houses along Pennsylvania Avenue. He regarded secessionists as traitors and despised them, saying, "The only good use for traitors is to hang them. They are worth more dead than alive."

After the firing on Fort Sumter, Scott ordered Robert E. Lee to report to him in Washington. Years earlier, Scott had referred to Lee as "the best soldier I ever saw in the field." And he had expressed a hope that Lee would one day take his place as general in chief. Scott and Lee talked for three hours in Scott's office. No one knows exactly what passed between them, except that Scott wanted Lee to command the Union armies and Lee obviously declined. Scott probably did not expect the Virginia-loving Lee to fight against the South. What he might have hoped (maybe) was that Lee would head a Northern army so formidable that there might never be a war. When Lee resigned from the United States Army and went home to Virginia, he wrote Scott, "I shall carry to the grave the most grateful recollections of your kind consideration, and your name and fame will always be dear to me."

The first Confederate victory, First Manassas in July 1861, was the "picnic battle," in which many Union notables drove out with their lunches to see what they assumed would be a Union victory. Southerners were overjoyed that the Virginia cavalry captured Winfield Scott's carriage and its six horses, Scott's sword and epaulettes, and silver, champagne, and other delicacies intended to celebrate what did not occur.

Scott had his military master plan, which he confided to his protégé, George McClellan. The West was important, Scott felt, since the South depended on the trans-Mississippi region for its produce and meat. He proposed blockading the Southern ports while a powerful Union force drove down the Mississippi Valley, occupying it and leaving behind strong forts. That would "squeeze the South to military death." McClellan called it "Scott's boa constrictor plan," but the press changed it to the "Anaconda Plan." They ridiculed it and carried public opinion with them. On the other hand, editor Horace Greeley's cry of "On to Richmond!" struck exactly the right chord with Yanks. So McClellan concentrated on subduing Virginia (and had no success doing it).

Old Scott and young Mac were both vain and self-confident. Eventually, their disagreements were settled by Scott's retirement. On November 1, 1861, Lincoln accepted Scott's application for retirement and appointed McClellan to take his place. Scott's departing promise was this: "Wherever I may spend the remainder of my life, my frequent and latest prayer will be, 'God save the Union.'" McClellan, not wanting to appear a complete ingrate, rose with his staff at four in the morning to escort Scott to the station. The older general was touched.

In retirement, Scott still had definite opinions about the Confederacy. "I am amazed that any man of judgment should hope for the success of any cause in which Jefferson Davis is a leader. There is contamination in his touch," he said. And he suggested this approach to the Rebels: "Say to the seceded states, 'Wayward Sisters, depart in peace!'"

In fact, the Lincoln administration finally decided the best approach to the war was (surprise!) Winfield Scott's Anaconda Plan, which worked. Scott was also right on another score: unlike dreamers North and South, he predicted the war would not be short, but rather a struggle in which the South would be subdued only after four years of fighting.

A curious note: two Civil War generals were named for the great and venerable Scott, Winfield Scott Featherston (South) and Winfield Scott Hancock (North).

The old general died, appropriately, in West Point, New York.

$\mathcal{R}$aphael Semmes, Confederate Admiral
(1809–1877)

RAIDER OF THE LOST CAUSE

"OLD BEESWAX" was his nickname, and any picture of the Confederacy's most famous sea hawk can tell you why—Semmes was known for his upturned (thanks to beeswax) mustache. More notably, he was the South's greatest plunderer of Yankee merchant ships.

Semmes grew up on a tobacco plan-

tation in Maryland and was sailing boats on the Potomac River from early childhood. He had a dual career as a sailor and a lawyer. He gained naval fame in the Mexican War when he almost drowned in a storm off the Mexican coast. The Maryland boy then settled in the port city of Mobile, Alabama. When that state seceded, he went with it, resigning from the United States Navy.

Old Beeswax could see that the Confederate navy was no match for the Union's. But if David could lick Goliath, then surely the South could lick the North (or at least do it some serious hurt). The Confederate government gave Semmes a task he relished: Do the enemy's commerce the greatest injury in the shortest time. He was to hurt the North by attacking and destroying its merchant ships (and seizing their cargoes, of course). Aboard the CSS *Sumter*, he captured seventeen Union merchant ships in six months. But it was another ship that made a name for itself and for Semmes.

The Confederacy had to have its ships built abroad, mostly in England. Britain prohibited the building of warships for other nations, so Confederate agents wisely contracted for English shipbuilders to construct "merchant vessels" (wink, wink), though the South had every intention of using them to attack Union ships. Union diplomats knew what was going on but could prove nothing. Built near Liverpool, the sleek vessel designated 290 slipped out of the harbor in July 1862 before the Federals could gather the evidence they needed. The 290 became famous as the CSS *Alabama*. In less than two years of cruising the world's oceans, it captured sixty-five Yankee ships (including five whalers sunk in New England waters) that had a value of about $6.5 million. Northern shippers greatly feared the infamous "Terror of the Seas."

Due to the Union blockade, Semmes could not send captured ships back to Southern ports, so he generally—but not always—burned them. Sometimes, he took them to neutral ports. On one occasion, he arrived in Cuba with seven Union ships in tow. Another time, he captured the USS *Sea Bride* off the South African coast, then sold it to an English merchant. He captured the *Conrad*, armed it, and turned it into another commerce raider, the *Tuscaloosa*. (Note how the Alabama resident bestowed Alabama names on his ships.)

Semmes was a merciful man and generally dealt kindly with the Yankee crews he captured. He would bring them aboard the *Alabama* before burning their ships, then release them at some neutral port. Still, Union agents were furious at the English for building the predatory ship and letting it loose on the seas. Secretary of State William Seward hinted at war if the English continued to construct ships like the *Alabama*. And the North despised Semmes as a mere pirate. The United States Navy offered a reward of half a million dollars for his capture. The owners of many

RAPHAEL
SEMMES

1809–1877

merchant ships began a "flight from the flag," registering their ships in foreign countries so they could escape Semmes's attention by *not* flying the United States flag.

The *Alabama* met its doom in the English Channel off Cherbourg, France, on June 19, 1864. It had gone to Cherbourg for repairs. While there, Semmes sent a challenge to the captain of the USS *Kearsarge*: "If you will give me time to recoal, I will come out and give you battle." The Union ship wore a kind of chain-mail armor. After a one-hour battle, the gallant *Alabama* sank to the bottom of the sea. Among the huge crowd that had gathered on the cliffs of northern France to watch was French master artist Édouard Manet, who immortalized the battle on canvas. The Yankee sailors were pleased at sinking the legendary raider, but they were so impressed with Semmes and his gritty crew that they refused to cheer as the *Alabama* went down. Semmes, who had a theatrical touch, threw his sword into the sea and was picked up by an English yacht, whose skipper garnered an official thanks from the Confederate Congress. On the other side of the Mason-Dixon line, the captain of the *Kearsarge* received the official thanks of the United States Congress. (As in *Alice in Wonderland,* prizes for everybody.)

Oddly, at war's end, the famous sea hawk became a landlubber. Though Semmes was by then rear admiral of the Confederate navy, Jefferson Davis made him a brigadier general in the Confederate army and told him to defend Danville, Virginia. By that time, the South needed generals worse than it needed sea raiders. Semmes was with General Joe Johnston when he surrendered to Sherman in North Carolina.

In December 1865, Old Beeswax was brought to Washington and (to no one's surprise) charged with piracy and treason. He was also charged with fleeing after surrendering at the *Alabama-Kearsarge* battle. The charges were eventually dropped, no doubt because Semmes the lawyer had seen to it that all his wartime deeds were technically legal and aboveboard.

The man the Yanks considered a glorified pirate made some money after the war by thrilling audiences with his lectures on "The Cruise of the *Alabama.*"

He returned to Mobile, where he practiced law and wrote *Memoirs of Service Afloat during the War Between the States.* The city of Mobile was so fond of Old Beeswax that it presented him with a fine home.

William Seward, Union Politician
(1801–1872)

SECRETARY SLY

SEWARD IS ONE of history's great almosts. In 1860, the well-known antislavery senator (deeply hated by Southern slave owners) almost won the Republican presidential nomination. It went to a dark horse, a lanky Illinois hick named Lincoln, since the Republicans did not believe the distinguished but colorless Seward could ever be elected. Seward, a former governor of New York, bore a slight grudge (and an overwhelming feeling of superiority) toward Honest Abe, even when Lincoln made him secretary of state. The appointment was generous on Lincoln's part, since Seward had been a Stephen Douglas supporter.

Being a more than slightly snobby New York, Seward tried to outshine the yahoo president, sticking his sizable beak of a nose into military affairs. (Had no one explained to him that military matters fell under the Department of War, not the Department of State?) One of his fellow cabinet members wrote in his diary, "Seward encourages the President's self-distrust. . . . He runs to the President two or three times a day, gets his ear, gives him his tongue." In April 1861, Seward sent Lincoln a memo he called "Thoughts for the President." It stated bluntly that the administration was "without a policy either domestic or foreign." If he thought Lincoln could be so easily cowed into letting him run the government, he was mistaken.

As secretary of state, Seward proved hawkish. Early in the war, the Union blockade of Confederate ports existed mostly on paper, and the nations of Europe were eager to evade it when it served their interests. Seward made it clear that picking a fight with any nation in Europe would be all right with him, since it would help unify the Union. No such war ever developed (which was good, since the Union had its hands full fighting the Confederacy).

Rather stupidly, Seward believed at the war's beginning that "there would be no serious fighting after all; the South would collapse and everything be serenely adjusted." Strange words, because as a senator, Seward once admitted in 1858 that the slavery issue had led to an "irrepressible conflict between opposing and enduring forces, and it means that the United States must and will, sooner or later, become either entirely a slaveholding nation or entirely a free-labor nation." The phrase *irrepressible conflict* stuck in Southern throats and made Seward one of the South's symbols of Northern intolerance. (Seward's family had once owned slaves, a practice legal in New York State until 1827.)

Seward's greatest contribution to the war was his delicate handling of the troublesome *Trent* affair. Two Confederate diplomats were seized (illegally, as everyone knew) from the unarmed British mail ship *Trent* by a Union warship. The British were appalled, as was the Confederacy (naturally). The Union was in ecstasy, even though the action could have led to war with Britain (and even though seizing an unarmed mail ship was hardly a bold and heroic act). Seward first reacted like most Northerners, itching for another war with Britain. But falling back into his role as a sly lawyer, he found a way out: he released the two Rebel diplomats (which satisfied Britain) but announced that the action had *not* been illegal (which satisfied the Union). It worked.

WILLIAM
SEWARD

1801–1872

In the successful plot to assassinate Lincoln, the conspirators were unsuccessful in assassinating Seward. While Booth was assaulting Lincoln, a fellow conspirator, the hulking Lewis Powell, forced his way into Seward's home after his ruse of delivering medicine to Seward didn't work. Seward was in bed recuperating from a carriage accident. His jaw had been broken on both sides, and an iron frame held it in place. The metal saved him, deflecting the slashes of Powell's bowie knife aimed at his throat. (Powell's original intention was to shoot Seward, but his gun misfired.) When Powell dashed from the room, he yelled, "I'm mad! I'm mad!" (No one doubted him on that.) He then wounded four members of Seward's household, including his son, whose skull was fractured by Powell's pistol butt. Seward's daughter opened a window and yelled "Murder!" Powell fled, was caught, and was eventually executed with the other conspirators. Curiously, Seward had gone on record years earlier as saying that "assassination is not an American practice or habit, and one so vicious and so desperate cannot be engrafted into our political system." He was mistaken.

During Reconstruction, Seward was one of many Yankee politicians who appeared to back-pedal on the issue of rights for blacks. Unlike the South-hating Radical Republicans in Congress, Seward seemed willing to let the South find its own solutions in dealing with the newly freed slaves. He had once been the abolitionists' darling, but when the war ended, he stated that "the North must get over the notion of interference with the affairs of the South."

Seward is best known for a postwar action, a $7.2 million purchase of a desolate tract of frozen land that the Russians were only too happy to sell. The United States at large hardly noticed the purchase. Those who did were puzzled. That much money for "Seward's Icebox"? Alas! Alack! Alaska!

Time has sided with Seward, though. The 1867 purchase, called "Seward's Folly," was a bargain. Alaska still commemorates him on the last Monday in March.

$\mathcal{P}$hilip Sheridan, Union General
(1831–1888)

DEVASTATION, IN SHORT

THE YOUNG IRISH Catholic cavalry star from Ohio was five-foot-four—so short that his sword left a mark in the soil where he walked; Grant remarked that he could find Sheridan by looking for his sword tracks. Another observer described him as "a stumpy quadrangular little man, with a forehead of no promise and hair so short that it looks like a coat of black paint." The tall, lanky Lincoln said of him, "He is one of those long-armed fellows with short legs that can scratch his shins without having to stoop over." His head was such an odd shape that military caps would hardly stay on it, so he usually carried his cap in his hand (or wore the porkpie that became his trademark). But on his ebony charger, Rienzi, the diminutive man looked grand.

"Little Phil" was dreadfully shy, particularly around women. But the military brought out his aggression in a big way. He lied about his birthdate (by one year) to get into West Point. His devout Catholic family feared the academy and the army would turn him into (horrors!) a Protestant. While at West Point, he was suspended for a year for chasing his cadet sergeant with a fixed bayonet and beating him with his fists. Phil was one of the few key Civil War players who was not a Mexican War veteran (he was too young at the time of the conflict). But what he lacked in experience and age (and height), he made up for with guts, guts, and more guts.

When the war began, Little Phil held a boring post as quartermaster. After squabbling with his fellow officers, he was transferred (to their relief) to a post as colonel of the Second Michigan Cavalry, a move that led him to fame in several major battles in Tennessee, most notably at Murfreesboro, where he was credited with saving General William Rosecrans's army. Sheridan's forces were key players in defeating Braxton Bragg at Chattanooga, which brought him to the attention of the North's rising star, U. S. Grant.

After Grant was promoted to major general, he made Sheridan commander of all the cavalry in the Army of the Potomac. Little Phil reorganized the cavalry troops and sent them to battle at the Wilderness, Spotsylvania, and Cold Harbor. They severed vital communication lines around Richmond, sending fear through the Confederate capital. His men were also responsible for the death of Confederate cavalry icon Jeb Stuart at Yellow Tavern, a major blow to Southern morale. (Sheridan announced that the purpose of his cavalry raids was to "whip Stuart out of his boots." He did indeed.)

In August 1864, Grant made the notorious raider the commander of the Army of the Shenandoah. Sheridan's orders were to move the Confederates south and destroy any supplies that would aid them. Grant ordered him to "eat out Virginia clear and clean . . . so that crows flying over it will have to carry their provender with them." Little Phil obeyed—in spades. Southerners had good reason to despise him, for he laid waste the Shenandoah Valley—Virginia's breadbasket—with the same demonic thoroughness Sherman applied in Georgia.

Sheridan believed that cutting Virginia's supply of foodstuffs would help end the war swiftly. He would cheerfully rattle off how he destroyed over two thousand barns and

PHILIP
SHERIDAN

1831–1888

seventy mills and seized livestock and grain for his troops. The farmers of the valley watched in horror as their burning barns lit up the night skies. Many of the farmers were pacifist Mennonites, but that didn't faze Sheridan's men. This destruction took place in the fall, with winter coming on. One Virginia officer wrote, "The government of Satan and Lincoln sent Phil Sheridan to campaign in the Valley of Virginia." For years, Shenandoah Valley residents referred to Sheridan's visit as "the Burning."

Sheridan effectively destroyed the Confederate army in the Shenandoah Valley. Facing the troops of pugnacious Confederate general Jubal Early at Cedar Creek, Virginia, Sheridan turned a near-defeat into victory, aided by the fact that Early's men got distracted looting a Federal baggage train. (Funny how hungry men are so easily distracted.) Little Phil rode to the front to rally his troops, waving his cap and hollering, "We'll get a twist on these people yet! We'll raise them out of their boots before the day is over!" They did. The general-cheerleader was rewarded with an official Thanks of Congress and a promotion to major general. His charge to his division commanders—"I shall expect nothing short of success"—was widely quoted.

News of Sheridan's defeat of "Old Jube" sent Northern cities into ecstasy—parades, fireworks, the whole nine yards. A popular poem called "Sheridan's Ride" was read from platforms all over the Union—a great boon to Lincoln in his reelection bid. Lincoln was mightily pleased. He said he had always believed that a cavalry general ought to be six-foot-four, but that he now believed "five-foot-four will do in a pinch." Sheridan and his troops were at Appomattox when Lee surrendered to Grant.

Like many generals, Sheridan was notorious for his profanity. When another Catholic general, William Rosecrans (who took his faith a little more seriously), scolded him for his swearing, Little Phil replied, "Unless I swear like hell, the men won't take me seriously."

During Reconstruction, Sheridan vexed Southerners as much as he had during the war. As commander of the Fifth Military District (which encompassed Louisiana and Texas), he was so harsh that he was removed after six months. During his brief tenure, Sheridan incensed the proud Texans by declaring that if he owned Texas and hell, he would rent out Texas and live in hell. He was then sent west to do to the Indians what he had done to the South.

But the Union adored its diminutive destroyer. Sheridan, the vandal of Virginia, succeeded Sherman as commander in chief of the United States armies in 1884.

William Tecumseh Sherman, Union General

(1820–1875)

TOTAL WAR TRAILBLAZER

"WAR IS HELL," according to the ugly red-head who made those words a reality for much of the South. As *Gone With the Wind* (both the novel and the movie) made clear, Sherman's name sent fear and trembling throughout the South not just during the war but long afterward.

Curiously, Sherman (called "Cump"— short for Tecumseh—by family and friends) had many Southern connections. In his post–West Point years, he served at posts in Florida, South Carolina, and Georgia. When he returned to the South twenty years later on his mission of destruction, he put his knowledge of Southern geography to good use. The Yankee hellhound was human, however. In a wartime letter to his beloved daughter Minnie, he wrote, "Do not think that I feel in this war as I would if England were the enemy opposed to us in battle. I feel that we are fighting our own people, many of whom I knew in earlier years, and with many of whom I was once very intimate."

About the general's name: his father named him Tecumseh after the famous Shawnee Indian chief. When young Tecumseh Sherman was baptized years later, the priest performing the ceremony felt the boy needed a proper Christian name, so he tacked on William to Cump's given name.

Just before the war broke out, Cump was the head of Louisiana State Seminary (the forerunner of Louisiana State University). When Louisiana seceded in 1861, Cump was offered a commission in the Confederate army. The Ohio-born Sherman declined. After Fort Sumter, he took a command in the Union army.

Sherman's volatile temper (he was a redhead, remember) helped fuel newspaper stories that he was cracking under the strain of war. Cump wasn't insane, but the Confederacy had good reason to consider him the ultimate fiend. Mississippi's capital, Jackson, was known as "Chimneyville" after being torched by Sherman; plenty of chimneys remained, but not many buildings attached to them. In fact, there were Chimneyvilles wherever Sherman marched. The South also saw a lot of "Sherman's neckties"—Confederate rails that Sherman's troops heated and wrapped around trees, making them unusable.

The *London Times*, reacting to what Sherman did in Mississippi, called him "the modern Attila." In Columbia, South Carolina, the statehouse still has bronze stars marking the scars made by his cannon. Southerners noted that Sherman was "a mite careless with powder and fire." Humans suffered, as did their animals. The way Sherman's men treated livestock would set animal-rights activists howling today. What the Yanks could not take with them, they killed. To save ammunition for use on men, Sherman's troops sabered pigs and poleaxed horses and mules between the ears. Cump excused the slaughter, saying, "To make war we must and will harden our hearts." War became less gentlemanly and decidedly more *modern* under men like Sherman and Phil Sheridan.

Sherman claimed he would "make Georgia howl," and his total-war army succeeded in that aim. On the famous "March to the Sea," the notorious "bummers" of the Union army looted private residences (although some of

WILLIAM
TECUMSEH
<u>SHERMAN</u>

1820–1875

them learned, like the fictional bummer in *Gone With the Wind*, that Southern belles could be very protective of their homes and belongings). Sherman ordered Yankee bummers tied up by their thumbs, but looting went on anyway. He chose his Georgia route scientifically, studying 1860 census records to find which counties and towns could provide the best food for his troops—who burned what they could not carry with them.

Sherman's men were followed by a "flock of black sheep"—the name the papers gave to the horde of slaves (mostly women and children) who trailed the Union armies. Cump was not antislavery (though his brother, Senator John Sherman, was). Like most Southerners of the day, Cump believed blacks and whites could not exist together except as master and slave. That was ironic, considering how many blacks followed his army. Sherman was moved by the sight of the "black sheep," but they impeded his progress, so he left most of them behind. Not surprisingly, he was disgusted at the new policy of enlisting black men as Union soldiers. "It is not fair to our men to count negroes as equals," he said. He (and most other Yanks) were strongly opposed to having blacks as fellow soldiers.

Sherman wasn't all bad. He generously allowed pastors in occupied towns to pray for President Jefferson Davis; hardly a religious man, the skeptical Sherman stated, "Jeff Davis and the devil both need it." And the infamous march through Georgia could have been avoided altogether. Sherman made this proposal to Georgia's governor: his troops would spare Georgia any destruction *if* Governor Brown would withdraw Georgia's troops from the Confederate army. Brown didn't. Instead, he issued a plea for help in defending the state against Sherman. Few responded, and no wonder, since Sherman had sixty thousand destructive Yankees at his command. Sherman then proved his generosity in a unique way at Christmas 1864. Having ended his march through Georgia at Savannah, he offered the captured city as his Christmas gift to Lincoln.

In spite of his military success (or excess, some would say), Sherman took a beating in the Northern press. Union papers called him a traitor because he was willing to guarantee property rights to conquered Confederates.

Sometimes he could be impish. In front of General Oliver Howard, who was notoriously devout, Sherman once remarked, "Damned cold this morning!" Howard stiffened and replied primly, "Yes, general, it is *quite* cold this morning." Sherman responded with a torrent of *damns*, and Howard made a hasty exit.

When did the Civil War end? The usual

view is that it concluded with Lee's surrender to Grant at Appomattox, Virginia. That was actually the *first* major surrender. The second major surrender occurred farther south, near Durham, North Carolina, where Confederate general Joe Johnston surrendered to Sherman eight days later. Georgia and the Carolinas must have breathed a sigh of relief. With the white flag waving, the red-headed vandal could do no more damage.

When Grant became president in 1869, Cump was named general in chief of the armies. He published two volumes of memoirs, in case anyone wanted details about how to make total war on civilians. In the 1870s, he showed the Indians of the West the same sort of hellish tactics he had shown the South. He and Phil Sheridan, the ravager of Virginia's Shenandoah Valley, were the Union's two most prized killing machines.

Sherman the soldier refused to do what Grant (and hundreds of other Civil War officers) did. He wanted no part of politics. When the Republicans pushed him to run for president, Cump's curt reply went like this: "What do you think I am, a damned fool?" He had always detested the politicians, editors, and preachers on both sides who helped divide the country. "Civilians are far more willing to start a war than military men," he said.

Perhaps it was fitting, then, that Sherman waged war primarily on civilians.

Edmund Kirby Smith, Confederate General
(1824–1893)

FLORIDA'S NATURE BOY

PEOPLE OFTEN FORGET that the largest state in the Confederacy was Texas, and that anything important took place west of the Mississippi River during the Civil War. But in fact, a great deal was going on in the West, that vast area that many people referred to as "Kirby Smithdom." Its story, and Kirby Smith's, deserve to be better known.

He was one of many Confederate bigwigs named Smith (twenty-two generals in all). So, early in the war, he began signing his dispatches "E. Kirby Smith" (the normal practice would have been "E. K. Smith"). He was frequently referred to as "Kirby Smith." Some write it, wrongly, as the hyphenated "Kirby-Smith" (although it appears that way on his gravestone).

He was a Florida boy, born in the nation's oldest town, St. Augustine. "Ted" or "Ned," as his family knew him, loved the outdoors and the Florida sunshine. From an early age, he poured out on paper his appreciation of nature. Some of his letters sound like a cross between a *National Geographic* article and *Walden*, the products of a boy who was half scientist, half poet. Young Ned delighted not only in flowers and trees but even in the swaying of his mule's ears in the breeze. Had he not been a soldier, he might have made a fine nature poet.

His army career is a familiar story in these pages. He graduated from West Point (where he was known by his classmates as "Seminole") and served with distinction in the Mexican War. When the South seceded, Smith followed his home state out of the Union. His loyalty to the Confederacy took him away from Florida for most of the war—a good thing for seeing new parts of the American wilderness, but a bad thing given his sentimental attachment to Florida. (He once wrote, "Land of sun and flowers! Land of the orange and mockingbird! With all thy swamps and mosquitoes, I love thee still!")

Smith fully expected to become an old, bookish, nature-loving bachelor, but fate intervened in the form of a contest among several Virginia girls to sew some nice shirts for a "bachelor officer from Florida." One of those girls ended up marrying the Florida officer. Over the course of Smith's late marriage to his adored and adoring Cassie, the couple made up for lost time, producing eleven children.

The Florida man was a respected general noted for his devoutness. (As with Robert E. Lee, another Episcopal saint, Smith seasoned his letters both personal and official with references to "the Almighty" and "Providence.") On more than one occasion (usually when the war was going badly), he considered abandoning the soldier's life and becoming an Episcopal minister, but he always wound up concluding he was unworthy.

How did the western Confederacy become "Kirby Smithdom"? No one expected it. Smith sparkled at First Manassas (which led to his fame and promotion) and served the war's early years in Virginia, Tennessee, and Kentucky. (He fell in love with East Tennessee's natural beauty, calling the Smoky Mountains "the Switzerland of America.") Then in February 1863 came a fateful order from Richmond: "The command of Lieut. Gen. E. Kirby Smith is extended so as to embrace the Trans-Mississippi Department." In brief, Smith was to be the head honcho of every-

EDMUND
KIRBY
SMITH

1824–1893

thing west of the Mississippi—Texas, Arkansas, and part of Louisiana.

As the eastern Confederacy fell to the Federals, Smith's domain grew more and more isolated from the Confederate government; the situation became even worse after the Federals gained control of the Mississippi River. Unfortunately, most of the best fighting men from the district were shedding their blood in Virginia, Tennessee, and Georgia, which led Smith to observe that "the aged, the infirm, and the lukewarm constitute the mass of the population that remains." He summed up his situation nicely: "It is no bed of roses." Kirby Smithdom faced not only Union attack but also marauding bands of deserters and bushwhackers, as well as Comanche and Kiowa Indian raids on white settlements. And then there was the burden of feeding and sheltering the hordes of women and children fleeing from the eastern Confederacy. Toward war's end, he complained that he was "a general without troops."

Smith negotiated the South's "third surrender" on June 2, 1865, formally laying down the arms of the western Confederacy, though there wasn't much to lay down by that time. (Lee's surrender at Appomattox was the "biggie," followed by Joe Johnston's surrender to Sherman in North Carolina.) News moved slowly in those days, and it wasn't until June 19 that Texas blacks learned from Union troops that they were free. That day subsequently became "Juneteenth," the great holiday for Texas blacks, widely celebrated for decades and still observed today.

Like many Confederate leaders, Smith hightailed it out of the country, expecting the worst from the Union government. After months of exile in Mexico and Cuba, he was pardoned by President Andrew Johnson and rejoined his family.

Where does a nature-loving ex-Confederate (and a faithful Episcopalian) end his days? Smith moved to the Tennessee mountains and the tiny village of Sewanee, home of the Episcopal college known (appropriately) as the University of the South. The former military man used his clout to ensure that the school did *not* teach military science. The bald, white-bearded patriarch taught math there.

When he breathed his last in 1893, he was the last of the South's full generals to die. Florida thought highly enough of its distinguished general to place a statue of him in the National Statuary Hall in the Capitol in Washington.

Edwin M. Stanton, Union Politician
(1814–1869)

THE CRANK ON THE WAR MACHINE

"WHERE DID THAT LONG-ARMED baboon come from?" was Stanton's first remark on seeing Abraham Lincoln. It was 1856, and the two men—both lawyers—were taking part in a lawsuit in Ohio. They were on the same side, and they won. Back in Illinois, Abe mentioned to his law partner that he had been "roughly handled by that man Stanton." A few years later, the long-armed baboon and the rough handler were working together daily (and often nightly) as president and secretary of war.

The two could not have been more different—the tall, folksy, good-humored Lincoln and the dumpy, cranky, bespectacled (thick lenses to boot), foul-tempered

Stanton. Yet they had a common goal: winning the war. That was ironic in a way, since Lincoln had little military background and Stanton had none whatsoever. Yet Stanton found himself in charge of six hundred thousand Union fighting men. Many of them (the generals especially) despised him. Perhaps there is a natural antagonism between soldiers and lawyers. Stanton had been one of the most successful corporate attorneys in the nation.

For all his stodginess, Stanton had his quirks. As a child, he liked to play with snakes; he once sent a roomful of women into spasms by entering with two wriggling snakes around his neck. A year after his daughter Lucy died, Stanton had her dug up and cremated; he then kept her ashes in a metal box in his room. His first wife died in childbirth, and Stanton insisted on burying her in her wedding clothes; he went twice a week to decorate her grave. His hellacious temperament to the contrary, he claimed to be a devout Episcopalian and wrote a book called *Poetry of God*.

The cranky man was attorney general under James Buchanan before becoming a caustic and blunt critic of the new Lincoln administration. He referred to Lincoln as the "original gorilla." But Lincoln, not knowing (or perhaps not caring) what Stanton had called him, put him in the secretary of war slot in January 1862, replacing the inefficient and notoriously corrupt Simon Cameron. Stanton was known to be honest in finances and busy as a beaver in mating season. He also liked to bully professional soldiers (as is typical when civilians have authority over military men). One official described him as "a born tyrant" and said, "He likes to use official power to crush and destroy anybody who may happen to stand inconveniently in his way."

Despite his abrasiveness, everyone thought Stanton was an improvement over Cameron. After months of grousing about the Lincoln administration, he was now part of it. He must have wanted to be there, for his income went from fifty thousand dollars annually as a lawyer to eight thousand as secretary of war.

Lincoln admired the man's energy and was frequently in his company. There was no telegraph between the White House and the War Department, so every day, Lincoln walked to Stanton's office. The first thing he did was read the war bulletins. Sometimes, he returned before bedtime to read the latest news; on occasion, he stayed all night. Every once in a while, humor arose (always from Lincoln, since Stanton had nary a drop in him). For example, Lincoln decided that with so many Germans in the Union armies, he needed a German

EDWIN M.
STANTON

1814–1869

general and so asked for Schimmelfennig. Stanton told him there were better-qualified Germans, but Lincoln told him the name Schimmelfennig would "make up for any difference."

All in all, Stanton was a good administrator. His generals' criticisms bounced off him with no effect. Slow-moving George McClellan locked horns with Stanton many times. From the Peninsula, he wired the secretary, "I have lost this battle because my force was too small. . . . You have done your best to sacrifice this army." The bombastic McClellan did not last out the war as a general, but Stanton stayed.

With Old Abe's blessing, Stanton crafted the hated draft law of March 1863. It led to the worst riots in United States history in New York City that summer. With the advent of the draft, civilians despised the secretary as much as soldiers did.

The secretary of war did not think Washington was well defended. When Jubal Early's Confederate troops menaced the city in 1864, Stanton stashed his personal hoard of gold (over five thousand dollars' worth) in the home of one of his clerks. Stanton was tigerish on the outside but timid as a rabbit on the inside, going into a panic if he thought Confederates were anywhere near Washington.

Stanton uttered one of the great quotations of the Civil War as Lincoln drew his last breath. It was 7:22 in the morning on Saturday, April 15, 1865, and raining in Washington when Stanton spoke the immortal words, "Now he belongs to the ages."

A few days later, General Sherman extended generous terms of amnesty when Joe Johnston surrendered to him in North Carolina. The Sherman-Johnston treaty allowed for the Rebel soldiers to return home and deposit their arms in state arsenals, and it offered assurances that Washington would recognize the South's state governments—all very magnanimous. But shocked politicians in Washington were ready to overlook Sherman's services in bringing the war to an end. His gentleman's agreement with Johnston was repudiated, and Stanton raked him over the coals, saying he had no authority to negotiate an agreement with the Rebels. In reply, Sherman let loose a torrent of profanity, saying that the Union's meddlesome politicians had not been worth fighting for.

When Sherman and his troops were to march victoriously into Washington, Stanton tried to prevent the general from riding at the head of his army, but the new president, Andrew Johnson, overruled him. Sherman dismounted at the reviewing stand, shook hands with Johnson and Grant, then ignored Stanton's outstretched hand, saying, "I do not care to shake hands with clerks." No one pitied Stanton much for this famous slight.

The impeachment of Andrew Johnson stemmed from his sacking of Stanton, whom he (and many others) believed was no longer needed now that the war was over. A noted South-hater, Stanton was raring to use military might to bully the defeated Rebels.

Johnson couldn't abide Stanton's temper and saw him as the Radical Republicans' Trojan Horse in the cabinet. Johnson missed being removed from office by one vote. Stanton resigned.

The worn-out lawyer got one final pat on the head. The next president, Grant, nominated him to the Supreme Court. Four days after Congress approved the nomination, the old war crank died.

Alexander Hamilton Stephens, Confederate Politician
(1812–1882)

VERTICALLY CHALLENGED POL

"LITTLE ALECK" was a red-haired, freckle-faced gnome of a man. Plagued by constant health problems, Stephens never weighed more than ninety pounds and was a life-long bachelor. Born into poverty and or-phaned at age twelve, he was determined to be a success. He proved his mettle by graduating first in his class at the Univer-sity of Georgia.

While serving in the United States House of Representatives, Stephens sup-ported states' rights and slavery—but op-posed secession. After Lincoln's election in 1860, though, he signed Georgia's secession ordinance. While many Southerners were gleeful over secession, the wise little owl took a more sober view: "Mark me when I say that in less than twelve months we shall be in the midst of a bloody war."

Stephens was elected vice president of the Confederacy in 1861. Representing the new Rebel government, he embarked for Richmond to woo Virginia into the Confederacy. He promised that if Virginia joined her Southern sisters, the Confederacy would move its capital from Montgomery, Alabama, to Richmond. Virginia accepted.

As it turned out, that was one of Stephens's last constructive acts for the South. For the duration of the Civil War, he was mostly a thorn in the side of President Jefferson Davis. His infamous "Cornerstone Speech" infuriated Davis because it claimed that slavery was the cornerstone of the Confederacy. (Stephens's racial views certainly would not pass the PC test today.) He criticized Davis for instituting a draft (as if the Confederacy had a choice), for temporarily suspending habeas corpus, and for just about everything else. In one statement, Stephens described Davis as "weak and vacillating, petulant, peevish, obstinate." While he admitted Davis was "a man of good intentions," he made it clear to friends that he did not believe him fit to be president of the Confederacy. (Who was? Stephens himself, per-

haps?) He accused Davis of running roughshod over the sacred teachings of the Southern god they both worshiped, the late great John C. Calhoun of South Carolina, whose speeches and writings on states' rights were notorious fodder for secessionists.

Like the vice president of the United States, Stephens was expected to preside over his nation's Senate. But having no voice or vote there, he grew bored. He departed Richmond and lived for eighteen months in self-imposed exile at his Georgia home, Liberty Hill.

Yet he didn't lose interest in the Confederacy. He proposed to Davis that the South make peace overtures to the North, preferably after a stunning Confederate victory such as Chancellorsville, when Northern public opinion would be against continuation of the war. Alas, timing is everything. The Battle of Gettysburg was raging while Stephens made his way to Washington to meet with Lincoln. Following that Union victory, the Federals had no desire to talk peace with the South (though they would have gladly talked of Southern *surrender*, naturally). Curiously, Davis had intended to send Stephens with Lee's armies as they marched into Maryland and Pennsylvania. But Stephens did *not* think it fit to play the role of peace commissioner while accompanying an invading army. That was one of many cases where the stubborn Davis and the

ALEXANDER
HAMILTON
STEPHENS

1812–1882

equally stubborn Stephens locked horns.

While Stephens was sulking in Georgia, he and the governor received a proposal from Union general William T. Sherman to meet him in Atlanta to discuss terms of surrender. Sherman knew that Stephens and Governor Brown both detested Jefferson Davis, but he was wrong in assuming they would negotiate a surrender without consulting the Confederate government. They refused to meet him, and he subsequently made Georgia howl with his devastating "March to the Sea."

In February 1865, a Union politician hatched a crackpot scheme to have the United States and the Confederacy join forces to drive the French out of Mexico. As brothers in arms, Johnny Reb and Billy Yank would forget their differences, and all would be well. Lincoln actually liked the idea, and the Confederacy sent a delegation that included Stephens to the infamous Hampton Roads Conference. At the four-hour conference, held at Fort Monroe in Virginia, Stephens posed a sensible question to Lincoln: "Is there no way of putting an end to the present trouble?" The answer was a resounding no, for the simple reason that Lincoln insisted on talking about reunion, while Stephens insisted on talking about "our two nations." Had the Confederate delegates been a little less stubborn, they might have negoti-

ated a generous armistice with Lincoln. The conference failed, though it did gain Stephens one personal victory: Lincoln promised to release Stephens's nephew from a Federal prisoner-of-war camp.

As the war dragged on, Stephens left Virginia for good. It was probably no consolation to him that his face appeared on the Confederate twenty-dollar bill.

After the war, he was elected a United States senator from Georgia. The Republicans refused to give Southern senators their seats, so Stephens did what any former lawyer would do: he resumed his legal practice. The year before he died, he was elected Georgia's governor. More important for history, he wrote (like so many ex-Confederates) a self-justifying book. He called it *A Constitutional View of the Late War Between the States*. Only a lawyer would publish a book with such a title.

The name *War Between the States* is Stephens's greatest legacy. If he didn't coin the name, he at least helped popularize it. For many years, people preferred it to *Civil War*. (Southerners preferred it for obvious reasons. A *civil war* means a war within a nation, and the Southern view was that it was a war between separate nations.)

Georgians apparently thought highly of Little Aleck. His statue represents the state in the United States Capitol, and Liberty Hill is now a state park and museum. He is buried beside his half-brother, Linton, the one deep emotional attachment of his life.

Speaking of statues: Stephens is one of the few non-Virginians honored with a bust in the State Capitol in Richmond. Considering his antipathy for the Confederate government, this is one of many, many postwar ironies.

Thaddeus Stevens, Union Politician
(1792–1868)

ANGRY OLD MAN

WHOEVER COINED the name *damn Yankee* may have had Stevens in mind. No Union politician was more blatantly anti-South than Stevens, who made it his life's goal to stamp out slavery and punish anyone connected with it. (On a personal level, he had reason to love the slaves: his housekeeper and common-law wife was a mulatto woman, Lydia Smith.)

The South, as Stevens saw it, was a proud, arrogant region full of sin. Being sinful, it needed punishing. Southerners were wicked, and that was all there was to it. He wasn't the only Yankee who felt that way, but he had the political clout to make his opinions bear fruit. Stevens was chairman of the powerful Ways and Means Committee in the House of Representatives, and he used his influence to end the war as quickly as possible, so the South's real punishment could begin.

Curiously, Stevens despised clergymen, even though many abolitionist leaders were ministers. He referred to them as "reverend parasites." Stevens was notoriously smutty, and many of his remarks and anecdotes were never printed because they were too risqué. Yet he knew the Bible well, and images from it were sprinkled throughout his speeches. (He obviously neglected to study the parts about "Love thy neighbor" and "Judge not, that ye be not judged.")

The old crank did have some humor in him. When a woman admirer once asked him for a lock of his hair, he bowed gallantly and handed her his whole wig. On another occasion, an enemy (and he had many) faced him on a narrow sidewalk and sneered, "I never step aside for a skunk!" Stevens stepped around the man, saying, "Pardon me, but I always do."

The 1860s were a decade of genuinely ugly politicians. Lincoln was—on the outside, anyway. Many people found Stevens ugly inside and out. Southerners despised him for

obvious reasons, but even his Yankee colleagues found him unpleasant. Gaunt, pallid, clubfooted, beetle-browed, and sporting a dark wig that barely resembled human hair, Stevens was described by one House member as "a man with a conscience, but mostly a pain in the arse." A foreign journalist described him as "irascible, vindictive, and even dangerous." The old man was a master of vehement sarcasm who cut to shreds anyone who disagreed with him. Most of his fellow Republicans feared crossing him because he liked to "read out" of the party anyone who didn't share his anti-Southern sentiments.

At one point, Southerners had a bit of vengeance. During the invasion of Pennsylvania, Confederate general Jubal Early came upon the Caledonia Ironworks, owned by none other than Thaddeus Stevens. The ironworks manager, pleading for mercy, told Early that the factory operated in the red, so there was no advantage in destroying it. (Stevens was a notorious gambler, one of the reasons his ironworks hadn't made him richer.) Early destroyed the factory anyway, all the way to ground level.

Stevens pushed Lincoln on the subject of emancipation long before the president was ready. Lincoln had a certain admiration for Stevens, but he saw the cranky old fanatic as

THADDEUS
STEVENS

1792–1868

an extremist who was oblivious to the fact that most Southerners did *not* own slaves.

With the defeat of the Confederacy and Lincoln's assassination, Stevens was in his glory. He described the South as "conquered provinces" that had no right to the usual protections of the Constitution. He drafted a plan to divvy up Southern plantations and give the land to the freed slaves. The plan failed, but Stevens and his fellow Radical Republicans were still determined to ride roughshod over the defeated South. And if poor Andrew Johnson tried to show too much compassion, he would meet his political doom. Or so they planned. In the House, Stevens engineered a vote of 126 to 47 to impeach Johnson, and he zestfully carried the announcement of im-

peachment into the Senate. By one Senate vote, Johnson was spared removal. But if Stevens and company lost that battle, they won the war, because Reconstruction was every bit as humiliating to the South as they hoped.

Just a few days before his death, Stevens told someone, "My life has been a failure." Some fellow Republicans agreed. After his death, one Republican congressman stated, "The death of Stevens is an emancipation for the Republican Party."

On his tombstone were carved these words: "Equality of man before his Creator." (Did he really mean it? He certainly didn't see Southerners as equals.) At his own request, his grave was in a black cemetery.

James Ewell Brown "Jeb" Stuart, Confederate General
(1833–1864)

GILDED GALLIVANTER

"THE LAST CAVALIER" sits immortalized in bronze on Richmond's Monument Avenue. With his sword drawn, his cape spread wide, and a gaudy plume on his hat, Stuart epitomizes the gallant knight of the Old South. The true Jeb Stuart was that and more.

Jeb was in fact a mama's boy who seems to have dedicated his life to pleasing women—platonically, of course. He made a boyhood vow to Mama Stuart never to touch liquor (a common vow to mamas in those days), and he never did. Though he was totally faithful to his wife,

Flora, he soaked up female attention like a sponge. His jangling golden spurs, his red, silk-lined cape, his light French saber, and the gauntlets reaching almost to his elbows impressed soldiers in both armies, but Stuart's aim seems to have been to wow the ladies. He succeeded, and they showered him with tokens of affection. Ladies loved to twine roses around his horse's bridle.

His entourage was just as impressive. Some admirers gave him two setters, whom he named Nip and Tuck. His band of merry cavalrymen included the banjo-picking Joe Sweeney (known for his comic parody songs) and other colorful characters, all proud to be associated with the near-legendary Jeb. (Rare is the celebrity who is so well known that one name will suffice. Consider: Elvis, Madonna, Prince—and Jeb.) Stuart's staff also included John Esten Cooke, a relative of his wife. Stuart referred to Cooke (though not to his face) as "a bore," but Cooke was in fact a noted Confederate author who wrote sketches of famous Rebel commanders for *Southern Illustrated News* and is best remembered for his *Life of Stonewall Jackson*.

Was Stuart handsome? They say clothes make the man, and it was certainly true in Jeb's case. In his West Point days, fellow cadets gave him the sarcastic nickname "Beaut." He wasn't, but he had charisma and was a thoroughly likable character. His famous cinnamon-red beard (which covered a less-than-perfect face) became part of the Stuart legend.

Jeb loved his role as the "Jolly Centaur" and was the great cavalry hero of the South. His troops somehow managed to make a complete circle—undetected—around Union general George McClellan's men (the famous "Ride around McClellan"). Another brassy deed was his capture of the personal effects of egomaniacal general John Pope. That, like the "Ride around McClellan," was a great morale booster for the Confederates. On another occasion, Stuart's men captured the trunk of a Union officer and learned that it contained letters from both the officer's wife *and* his mistress. Seeing a chance to be moral and impish at the same time, Stuart mailed the mistress's letters off to the wife. On another occasion, he had one of his men send a telegraph to a Union officer complaining about the quality of the mules Stuart had just captured from the Federals.

A chatty, backslapping "people person," Stuart somehow became a close friend of the tight-lipped, reticent Stonewall Jackson. Perhaps opposites attract. One night, after a long day of riding, Stuart crawled into bed (with his spurs still on) beside the sleeping Jackson.

JAMES
EWELL
BROWN
"JEB"
STUART

1833–1864

In the morning, Jackson appeared at breakfast rubbing his scratched calves. According to one account, he requested that if Stuart ever slept with him again, his fellow general must not "ride him around like a horse all night." When Jackson was mortally wounded after his victory at Chancellorsville, Stuart was given temporary command of Stonewall's forces.

Historians claim the Civil War pitted brother against brother. In Jeb Stuart's case, it pitted father-in-law against son-in-law. Stuart's wife was the daughter of Union general Philip St. George Cooke, who also had to endure the fact that his son John Rogers Cooke became a Confederate general. The elder Cooke referred to his son and son-in-law as "those mad boys." As for Cooke's decision to stay with the Union, Stuart quipped, "He will regret it but once, and that will be continuously." The squabble in the Cooke family was good fodder for gossip in both the South and the North. Jeb had named his son for Grandpa Cooke before the war, but since Gramps was fighting on the wrong side, he rechristened the boy Jeb Jr. (A Civil War tidbit: the Union had a general named Philip St. George Cooke, while the Confederacy had one named Philip St. George Cocke.)

Despite his in-law problem, Stuart was liked by everyone—almost. He had a long-running feud with General William "Grumble" Jones, one of the few generals court-martialed during the war. Though a good commander, Jones was notoriously foulmouthed and crabby. As fate would have it, both he and Stuart were killed in action.

Like several other Confederate generals, Stuart died young. He once stated, "All I ask of fate is that I may be killed leading a cavalry charge." He got his wish—sort of. In fact, the shot that killed him was fired by a Union soldier *on foot.* After being mortally wounded, the ever-spunky Stuart said, "I had rather die than be whipped." A fighter to the end, he ordered his men, "Go back! Go back and do your duty, as I have done mine, and our country will be safe. Go back! Go back!"

Lying on his deathbed in Richmond, Jeb received numerous visitors, including President Jefferson Davis. The pious mama's boy died singing "Rock of Ages" with his devoted men. His last words: "I am going fast now. I am resigned. God's will be done."

The fatherly Robert E. Lee grieved at Stuart's death, noting, "He never brought me a piece of false information." Lee, who had been the head of West Point while Stuart was there and who called Jeb "the eyes of the army," later claimed, "I can scarcely think of him without weeping."

Charles Sumner, Union Politician
(1811–1874)

MAGNIFICENT OBSESSIVE

THE NEW ENGLAND PURITANS had a reputation (partly deserved, partly not) for taking life very, very seriously, with minimal joy and humor. Their hatred was directed at sin and the devil. Their descendants were less serious about Christianity but equally serious about politics and social issues—slavery in particular. Charles

Sumner was a Puritan descendant (Boston-born, of course) whose hatred was directed at slave owners and the South in general.

Sumner graduated from Harvard Law School and became a Boston lawyer and an antislavery spokesman. He loudly aired his belief that the Compromise of 1850 and the annexation of Texas were ploys by Southern politicians to extend slavery into new territories. "Mr. Abolition" was elected to the Senate in 1851 and became Congress's most vocal opponent of slavery. He claimed he dealt not in politics but in morals.

In May 1856, he delivered his famous "Crime against Kansas" speech, in which he denounced the Kansas-Nebraska Act (the brainchild of Senator Stephen Douglas of Illinois), along with Senator Andrew Butler of South Carolina, whom he accused of having a "mistress . . . the harlot, slavery." Sumner gave his speech to a packed Senate chamber. "My soul is wrung with the outrage, and I shall pour it forth," he said. Though Senator Butler himself was not present, the deliberately inflammatory speech irked Southerners, notably Congressman Preston Brooks, Butler's nephew. Brooks took his cane to Sumner on the Senate floor, beating him so savagely that the cane was reduced to splinters.

The so-called Brooks-Sumner Affair was one of the first events to be reported by telegraph—a new medium that made communications instantaneous for the first time in history. The incident was national news, and it helped solidify Northern opposition to slavery. The people of Massachusetts naturally re-elected Sumner, their almost-martyred icon, to the Senate. Before John Brown's hanging in

1859, Sumner was *the* abolitionist hero. While Sumner recuperated (it took him three years to do so), his empty chair in the Senate served as a reminder of the beating. Among Southerners, there was rejoicing over the near-death of the South's greatest foe. Many Southerners sent Brooks canes to replace the one he had broken to pieces on Sumner. One was engraved, "Hit him again!"

Sumner's fellow abolitionists in Congress found him eloquent and admirable but narrow-minded. He was six-foot-two, heavyset (*fat*, some said), distinguished, and (some said) "godlike" in his bearing. One political ally called him "a born Puritan character, an aristocrat," but one who had a "determination to impose his principles upon the world at any cost."

Once Lincoln was elected, Sumner urged him to immediately emancipate the slaves. Lincoln wasn't ready yet, though he respected Sumner. Lincoln, a man of the people, saw the complexities involved in fighting the war and freeing the slaves. Sumner saw no complexities; the war was about abolishing slavery, and that was that.

Sumner was the counterpart of Thaddeus Stevens in the House—a Radical Republican and a hater of everything Southern. He preached "Southern suicide"—the idea that the

CHARLES
SUMNER

1811–1874

seceding Confederate states had given up all claims to statehood. So, naturally, he opposed Lincoln's plan to eventually readmit the Southern states with a minimum of vindictiveness. He and Stevens both pushed for Reconstruction under congressional control (that is, under men devoted to punishing the South). He wanted to confiscate Confederate estates and distribute the land to former slaves. He led the move to impeach Andrew Johnson and was peeved that removal fell one vote shy.

Sumner's career was his whole life. Like many people without families and emotional anchors, he let his obsession rule him. Then, in 1866, the career-driven bachelor took a wife. (His mother had just died. Any connection?) He was fifty-five, and she was twenty-five and voluptuous—a trophy wife if there ever was one. Sumner wrote a friend, "Today I began to live." But the match made in heaven quickly became hellish. Sumner had lived too long as a bachelor and was vain and egotisti-

cal. His wife was a social butterfly, moving at a quicker tempo than her husband. They separated, then divorced. William Cullen Bryant might have had them in mind when he wrote, "A woman is not content with a husband who is exclusively occupied with himself and his own greatness."

The great South-hater died appropriately: he had a heart attack in the Senate chamber and succumbed the next day.

Mary Chesnut's wonderful Civil War diary has some insightful comments on Sumner and his fellow abolitionists, who lived "in nice New England homes—clean, clear, sweet-smelling—shut up in libraries, writing books which ease their hearts of their bitterness to us. . . . What self-denial do they practice? It is the cheapest philanthropy trade in the world—easy. Easy as setting John Brown to come down here and cut our throats in Christ's name."

Roger B. Taney, Chief Justice
(1777–1864)

DECISION BEFORE THE FIRE

HIS NAME IS pronounced *Tawny*, but historians have called him quite a few other names, none of them good. His chief claim to fame is the famous (or infamous) *Dred Scott* decision of 1857, in which the Supreme Court, with Taney at the helm, decided that blacks were not citizens—period. It sounds perfectly barbaric to us, and sounded so to many people in 1857 as well—but not to everyone, and certainly not to slave-owning Southerners, and certainly not to the pro-Southern Taney himself.

It could not have been otherwise. Taney grew up on a Maryland tobacco plantation and took slavery for granted.

Being the second-born son, however, he could not inherit the family spread (inheritance laws were strange in the old days), so he trained as a lawyer, did well in his practice, and married the sister of Francis Scott Key (the Maryland man who gave us "The Star-Spangled Banner"). His beloved Anna Key Taney gave him six daughters and a happy marriage, and the prosperous lawyer inevitably entered politics. He became a fervent supporter of Andrew Jackson, who made him the nation's attorney general in 1831. Later, Jackson quarreled with his secretary of the treasury, dismissed him, and gave the post to Taney (though the Senate disliked Taney so much that it never confirmed him in that position). In 1836, the loyal Jackson gave him the job of a lifetime, chief justice of the Supreme Court, where he succeeded the famous John Marshall of Virginia, who had just died. Jackson detested Marshall and was glad to replace him with a man after his own heart. As chief justice, Taney administered the oath of office to nine presidents, the last being Abraham Lincoln in 1860.

He and the Supreme Court were fortunate, because throughout the 1840s and 1850s, the issue of slavery mostly passed them by. But a case fell into their lap in 1856 that had to be dealt with. Dred Scott, a Missouri slave, had been taken by his master into the free states of Illinois and Wisconsin. Scott sued for his freedom on the grounds that he was in territory where he was no longer a slave. Could he, the Supreme Court was asked, legally sue for his freedom? The nine justices each wrote separate opinions in the case, but Taney spoke for the majority when he wrote that a slave was not a United States citizen and thus could not sue in federal court, and that residing in a free state did not automatically free a slave. Reading his opinion aloud, the eighty-one-year-old Taney noted that the Declaration of Independence stated that "all men are created equal." Taney said that those words "would seem to embrace the whole human family. . . . But it is too clear for discussion that the enslaved African race were not intended to be included."

The conclusion of *Dred Scott v. Sandford* made the South happy and sent Northern abolitionists into a tailspin. Public opinion of the Supreme Court hit a low in the North, at least among the elite. Abolitionists were convinced that slavery would never be abolished unless Congress amended the Constitution. Renowned newspaper editor Horace Greeley called Taney's views "wicked," "atrocious," "abominable," "false," etc. The *Chicago Tribune* observed, "We scarcely know how to fathom the wicked consequences which may flow from it."

Taney was a devout Catholic free from

ROGER B.
TANEY

1777–1864

scandal and respected for his integrity and personal warmth. Despite the North's assumption that he was proslavery, he in fact had freed the slaves he inherited. When he wrote his fifty-four-page decision in the *Dred Scott* case, he thought he was protecting the legitimate interests of a minority (Southerners) against the majority (Northerners)—a valid idea, except that another minority (blacks) counted for nothing.

Did Taney have any idea on March 4, 1860, when he administered the oath of office to Lincoln, what his decision had meant to the nation? One observer wrote that on that day, Taney had "the face of a galvanized corpse." His hands shook with age (or was it emotion?) as he held the Bible for Lincoln, the "black Republican" whose election had set the Southern states running toward secession. In his much-quoted "House Divided" speech in 1858, Lincoln had called Taney's opinion in the *Dred Scott* case part of a conspiracy to extend slavery nationwide.

When the Civil War was in full swing, the North looked with suspicion on the Southern-sympathizing Taney. He and Lincoln locked horns not over the issue of slavery but over Lincoln's cavalier attitude toward habeas corpus. Lincoln was only too happy to suspend the honored practice when suspected traitors in the North were being investigated, but Taney sided with tradition and argued that while the war might be a national emergency, the president had no right to trample on habeas corpus. In *Ex parte Merryman*, he wrote a strong case for the rights of civilians in wartime, and Southern newspapers widely and eagerly reported that showdown between president and chief justice.

Time and age removed Lincoln's problem when Taney died in Washington in October 1864. Lincoln replaced him with the decidedly antislavery Salmon P. Chase.

History is full of ironies. Taney was a quintessential nice guy—honest, deeply religious, devoted to his family, charming in a distinctively Old South fashion. He was also a darn good lawyer and judge. Yet his name will be forever linked with one of the Supreme Court's most famous—and worst—decisions. The fateful *Dred Scott* case gave new energy to the abolitionists and led to a war that must have given Taney much grief.

George H. Thomas, Union General
(1816–1870)

THE VIRGINIA YANKEE

How would the Confederacy have fared without its great Virginia generals? There were so many, and they were such luminaries. In 1861, the United States Army saw plenty of fine Virginia officers resigning their commissions and heading home to the Old Dominion.

One didn't. He was George Henry Thomas, born in southeastern Virginia's "Black Belt" (so called because slaves outnumbered whites three to two in that region).

Thomas's home county experienced the bloody horror of Nat Turner's slave rebellion. Legend has it that during Turner's revolt, young George rode from house to house warning the white inhabitants. It wasn't so, although the Thomas family did have to vamoose from Turner's bloodthirsty band. The family's slaves must have been treated well, for they flatly refused to aid Turner.

At West Point, Thomas (one of many Virginia lads) was the possessor of several nicknames. One was "Old Pap" (he looked like one). His roommate, William Tecumseh Sherman, called him "Old Tom" (at age twenty-four, Thomas was the oldest cadet in the class of 1840). William Rosecrans called him "George Washington" because of his Southern dignity and formality. The gregarious, lanky Sherman and the shy, portly Thomas were bosom buddies. One classmate said that Thomas followed Sherman around like a loyal St. Bernard. It was a classic pairing of the life of the party with the personality-deprived. The chatty Sherman drew people to him; when Thomas gave a fireside chat, the fire went out.

In the Civil War's early days, Sherman asked Lincoln to appoint Thomas as a general. Lincoln was impressed with Thomas but doubted his loyalty, since most Virginians put their state ahead of the Union. Sherman replied, "Mr. President, Old Tom is as loyal as I am, and as a soldier he is superior to all on your list." Lincoln then asked, "Will you be responsible for him?" Without hesitation, Sherman replied, "With the greatest pleasure." Lincoln sent his nomination of Old Tom as a brigadier general to the Senate.

Old Tom was required (like all officers) to renew his oath of allegiance to the United States government in April 1861. He remarked, "I don't care; I would just as soon take the oath before each meal during my life if the department saw fit to order it."

At age thirty-six, Thomas married a woman from New York State. When he threw in his lot with the North, his spinster sisters in Virginia, Judith and Fanny, turned his picture to face the wall, destroyed his letters, and requested that he change his last name. They believed his Yankee wife had turned him against his native state. The people of his home county, Southampton, said they would hang him if he ever came home. He never did.

Once, after a battle, Thomas was asked if the dead should be buried in plots for the different states they hailed from. He replied, "No, no. Mix them up. I am tired of states' rights."

Thomas was as reticent and humorless as Stonewall Jackson, on one occasion saying, "I have educated myself not to feel." Heavyset and quiet, he struck many people as sluggish, though he wasn't. At Murfreesboro, during a

GEORGE H.
THOMAS

1816–1870

council of generals, Rosecrans asked Thomas to protect a proposed retreat, and Thomas hurriedly responded, "This army can't retreat." Those words were Old Tom's slogan. He became a hero to all the North—the "Rock of Chickamauga"—in September 1863 when he and his troops held their ground after the rest of the Union line folded. Though that fateful Georgia battle was a spirit-lifting victory for the Johnny Rebs and the undoing of Rosecrans, it made Thomas's reputation.

But in a few Yankee minds, there were still doubts about Old Tom's loyalties—or at least about his abilities as a fighter. Grant thought him too slow and wanted to relieve Thomas of his command in Tennessee. Lincoln resisted, but Grant insisted, and Lincoln let him have his way. Grant telegraphed the order to Thomas, but an ice storm delayed communications. Before Grant could notify Thomas that he was sacked, Thomas attacked John Hood at Nashville. Lincoln then telegraphed Thomas, "You made a magnificent beginning; a grand consummation is within your reach. Do not let it slip." He didn't. Bits and pieces of Hood's army escaped, but for all practical purposes, it ceased to be an army. Lincoln's faith in Thomas was rewarded. Grant had been wrong. Newspapers reported that the Rock of Chickamauga had become the Sledge of Nash-

ville. Old Tom was made a major general.

Though unemotional and chilly, Thomas had real affection for his soldiers, who called their fleshy, graybearded general "Old Pap" and "Old Slow Trot."

For obvious reasons, the Virginia-born Union hero did not wish to settle in the South after the war. In fact, toward the end of his life, he was sent as far as possible from the whole Civil War scene—to the Pacific coast. He died in San Francisco. He was not buried in Virginia, but in his wife's hometown of Troy, New York.

Thomas's death came in 1870, before former Civil War generals began publishing memoirs that served mainly to praise themselves and blame others. Even had he lived longer, Old Tom probably would not have contributed to the glut. He once stated, "My private life is my own, and I will not have it hawked about in print for the amusement of the curious."

In his Mexican War days, Thomas (still a loyal Virginia boy at that time) had so distinguished himself that the residents of Southampton County gave him a beautiful gold-and-silver saber (made in the North— was that some kind of omen?). He treasured the gift but wore it on only one occasion— his wedding. When he sided with the Union and left Virginia, the saber stayed behind. In 1900, thirty years after his death, Judith, his still-bitter sister, gave it to the Confederate Memorial Institute in Richmond. She claimed that "General Thomas had many friends, a comfortable home, and a native state until he deserted them."

Today, a bronze equestrian statue of the Virginia Yankee sits in the center of Thomas Circle in Washington.

Robert A. Toombs,
Confederate Politician and General
(1810–1885)

MR. BIG (AND ALMOST MR. PRESIDENT)

THE NAME *TOOMBS* has a hulking, heavy sound, and Robert Toombs was a massive man physically and politically. The bulky, loose-jointed man had fierce eyebrows, baggy eyes, and heavy jowls. Yet he was anything but slow and lazy. In fact, he had a kind of restless energy, a "new South" feel before the New South existed. He was part of a class new in Southern life. Professional men such as lawyers, bankers, doctors, and businessmen were adding a healthy variety to the mix of rich planters, poor whites, and slaves. (Everyone forgets about another class, the many respectable small-scale farmers who were neither "white trash" nor planters, but that is another story.)

Like many men in the new class, Toombs went into politics. A Georgian, he was a successful courtroom lawyer famous for his persuasive speeches to juries. He worked his way up through the state legislature, then the United States House, then the Senate. In the Senate, he was a proslavery spokesman who resented the "meddling" and the abolitionist leanings of his Northern colleagues. He, Jefferson Davis of Mississippi, and Robert M. T. Hunter of Virginia were known as the Senate's "Southern Triumvirate" of powerhouse proslavery orators.

Following Lincoln's election, Toombs joined the secessionist ranks. He gave his farewell speech in the Senate, proclaiming, "The Union, sir, is dissolved." He then swaggered out of the Capitol and over to the Treasury Department, demanding whatever Senate pay he was due, plus funds to pay his way back to Georgia.

When delegates met in Montgomery to form the Confederacy, the man everyone knew as Bob Toombs was on the short list for president. Unfortunately, Bob was noted for being fond of the grape. According to one observer, he was "tight every day at dinner" in Montgomery. Shortly before the election, he became *very* drunk. So the just-born Confederacy chose the decidedly sober Jefferson Davis, who was pruning rose bushes at his Mississippi plantation when he received the official message that he was president. The message was signed by Robert Toombs. Big Bob never quite got over the defeat.

Even so, when the Confederate government moved from Montgomery to Richmond, Toombs was aboard the presidential train that gave Southerners a chance to greet their new president. Gung-ho secessionist Louis T. Wigfall was there, too. Hailed by admiring, cheering crowds at each whistle stop, that was probably the most pleasant time Davis, Toombs, and Wigfall (all former United States senators) had during the war. Amidst all the good feeling, Toombs might have been able to temporarily forget that he had strongly advised against firing on Fort Sumter, predicting that it would ignite a war. His advice was wise but went unheeded.

As a consolation prize for not being president, Toombs was made secretary of state, a curious position in a nation that wasn't (in the world's eyes) quite a nation yet. An Englishman asked Toombs, "Where will I find the State Department?" "In my hat, sir," Toombs replied, "and the archives are in my coat pocket." Toombs, like Jefferson Davis, had no

ROBERT A.
TOOMBS

1810–1885

doubt read David Christy's 1855 book, *Cotton Is King: Or, Slavery in the Political Economy,* which gave the South its misguided "Cotton Is King" slogan and was the basis of "cotton diplomacy." Christy's followers were mistaken in their optimistic belief that the South's abundant cotton gave it clout on the world scene. They expected that the nations of Europe would force the Union to lift its blockade of Southern ports so that cotton could reach Europe. One important point: Both France and England had a huge surplus of cotton in their warehouses. So cotton was definitely not king. But the Confederacy was in dire need of supportive illusions, and this was one of the favorites.

Toombs didn't stay long as head of the State Department—only until July 1861, when he resigned in the hope that he could do more good (and channel his churning energy) as a general. Both North and South suffered much at the hands of their political generals, and Toombs fit the mold: lots of ambition, lust for glory, but little ability. Like many political generals, he despised the professional officers, the West Pointers (which was nothing but plain envy, of course). He once claimed that the Confederate army's epitaph would read, "Died of West Point." In fact, Toombs's brigade fought fairly well at Antietam, where he himself was wounded. He expected a promo-

tion and did not get it, so (to no one's surprise) he resigned.

He went home to Georgia to grouse about the stupidity and incompetence of Jefferson Davis and the entire Confederate government (which, he knew, would have blossomed had *he* been president). Mary Chesnut wrote in her famous wartime diary, "Toombs is ready for a revolution. He curses freely everything Confederate." The peevish man was elected to the Confederate Senate but refused to serve. He found a fellow griper in Vice President Alexander Stephens, also a Georgian living in sulky self-exile. The two and Georgia's notorious governor, Joe Brown, formed a kind of pouty anti-Davis trio. Brown made Toombs a colonel of the Georgia militia and sent him to try to thwart Sherman's invasion. Like everyone else who opposed Sherman, Toombs had no luck.

Even near the war's end, he still had some bombast in him, saying the South could "whip forty Yankee nations." He was mistaken: it could not whip one.

As a former United States senator, Toombs feared being tried for treason once the Union won the war. He skedaddled to Paris, where he lived until 1867. Then he returned to his successful law practice and to wielding influence in Georgia politics. Note: He had pull—probably more than anyone else in the state—*but could not hold elected office.* Toombs was an "unreconstructed Rebel" to his dying day. Since he would not apply for a pardon and take the oath of loyalty to the United States, he was barred from holding office. Technically, he was never again an American citizen. Supposedly, he said to some Yanks, "Pardon for what? I haven't pardoned you-all yet!" Even if the quote isn't quite true, it certainly sums up his attitude (and that of all the "unreconstructeds").

He never let up in his hatred for Yankees. One story (true or apocryphal, who knows?) says that Toombs was in the local telegraph office when it received news of the great Chicago fire in 1871. A crowd gathered outside, and Toombs passed on the news about the heroic firemen and volunteers. Then the old unreconstructed Rebel added with a smile, "But the wind is in our favor."

Elizabeth Van Lew, Union Spy
(1818–1900)

METHOD IN HER MADNESS

WHEN DIZZY LIZZIE Van Lew was buried in a Richmond cemetery, her grave initially went unmarked, and for good reason: local people loathed her. Operating under the code name "Mr. Babcock," she had fed military information about the Confederates to some key players in the Union, notably U. S. Grant. Known to locals as "Crazy Bet," she was notorious for hiding escaped Union prisoners of war in her home, taking food and gifts (and money to bribe guards) to Union prisoners, buying and freeing slaves, and generally doing everything in her power to vex the Confederacy and her native state.

When the Civil War began, most

Virginia officers in the United States Army resigned their commissions and came scurrying back to Old Virginny, as did the state's representatives and senators in Congress. Elizabeth Van Lew was the cream of Richmond. She lived in a fine home on Church Hill and was exactly the sort of woman who would despise Yankees, abolitionists, and other evil folks. What turned her against the South?

Blame it on the Yankees. She had gone to school in Philadelphia and soaked up abolitionism from a governess. When her father died, she persuaded her mother to free the family's nine slaves (and to buy the slaves' relatives and free them as well). Word of her abolitionist sympathies spread, and the pretty Richmond belle found herself invited to fewer and fewer parties and dinners. Richmonders remembered that Bet's father was originally from New York. So even though Bet herself was Richmond-born, her family had (horrors!) Yankee roots.

She was already a confirmed spinster in 1859 when Virginia trembled at John Brown's raid on Harpers Ferry. Unlike her fellow Richmonders, who saw Brown as the devil incarnate, Crazy Bet hailed him as a saint and hero. When war came in 1861, she began using some of her family's lands as relay points for passing on information to the Federals at Fort Monroe, a hundred miles east.

Why did the former belle become known as "Crazy Bet"? She knew that loyal Confederates were suspicious of her, so she decided to play the role of a ditzy—and therefore *harmless*—eccentric. She dressed in a huge calico bonnet, buckskin leggings, and other poor-white garb and walked the streets with her head cocked to one side, singing nonsense songs and mumbling to herself. (Since she was a Yankee sympathizer, her sanity was already in doubt.) The impression she gave was that of a kooky old spinster.

Dizzy Lizzie was no fool. She sent information (written in code) in hollowed-out eggs, the soles of her servants' shoes, the spines of books, and other nooks and crannies. Using such hidey-holes, she got information to and from Union soldiers imprisoned in Richmond. When she visited Federals in Libby Prison (a converted tobacco warehouse) and other Richmond prisons, she came across as a nice, loyal lady (if slightly batty) bringing books and food (like a basket of eggs). But when those prisoners were exchanged and sent back north, they often took with them information passed on by Crazy Bet.

Her masterwork came in using Mary Elizabeth Bowser, an educated black woman, as a spy in the household of the president himself,

ELIZABETH
VAN LEW

1818–1900

Jefferson Davis. Bowser played the role of a competent (but slightly dumb and completely illiterate) servant extremely well and passed on to the Federals all the information she gathered from serving the Davises.

Van Lew's house had (as many people suspected) at least one secret room where she harbored runaways from the city's prisons. One of her guests was her brother, who had been drafted (much against his will) into the Confederate army. He quickly deserted and hid out in Bet's home for a time.

Crazy Bet was the guiding spirit behind one of the boldest plots of the war, the Dahlgren raid on Richmond. Colonel Ulric Dahlgren and his men aimed to free the Union prisoners in Richmond, assassinate President Davis and his cabinet, and torch the city. The plot was foiled, and Dahlgren was killed by Rebels and dumped in a shallow grave. Bet (who felt responsible for his death) had him dug up and given a proper (and secret) burial. After the war, she notified the Dahlgren family of the grave site. It was a long time before the Union even admitted approving the Dahlgren raid.

Needless to say, Dizzy Lizzy was ecstatic when the Yankees took Richmond. While the city burned, some of her many enemies threatened to wreak their vengeance on the old trai-

tor. Lizzy told them, "General Grant will be in town in about an hour. You do one thing to my home and all of yours will be burned before noon!" They backed down. At her home, she raised the first American flag flown in Richmond since 1861. Grant called on his favorite correspondent, who had him to tea. For the rest of her life, she kept Grant's calling card as a treasured memento. After his election as president, he made her postmistress of Richmond. The defeated Confederates were not pleased. One Richmond newspaper stated, "We regard the selection of a Federal spy to manage our post office as a deliberate insult to our people."

Bet had been hated but mostly ignored during the war. Postwar, Richmonders hated her even more. They learned that she had paid arsenal workers to sabotage munitions—which had led, no doubt, to the deaths of Confederate soldiers. Adults told children she was a witch and urged them not to walk on her side of the street. When her mother died, Bet could not find enough friends to serve as pallbearers. She claimed that her church, the historic St. John's Episcopal, even locked her out of its worship service.

Richmonders had their revenge in another way. After Grant's eight years as president, she lost her position as postmistress and found herself in dire financial straits. Several former Union officers remembered her loyalty (or *treachery*, as the South saw it) and enabled her to keep the wolf from her door. But she became increasingly eccentric in her old age, so her Crazy Bet routine was no longer an act.

Years after her death, some Yankee friends erected a marker on her grave. The inscription read, "She risked everything that is dear to man—friends, fortune, comfort, health, life itself, all for one absorbing desire of her heart—that slavery might be abolished and the Union preserved."

Richmond had a different opinion.

Gideon Welles, Union Politician
(1802–1878)

A CONNECTICUT YANKEE
IN ABE LINCOLN'S COURT

WHEN PEEVISH, highly opinionated people keep diaries, their words are usually worth reading (though not necessarily true in every detail). One of the great diaries of the Civil War was kept by a member of Abraham Lincoln's cabinet, a man who never lacked for an opinion on any subject, the irritable (but very readable) Gideon Welles. Through his jaundiced eyes, we get priceless glimpses of Lincoln, the cabinet, leaders of Congress, and a parade of generals good and bad.

Gilbert and Sullivan's ever-popular operetta *H.M.S. Pinafore* features an admiral of the English fleet who rose to his position through political connections, but who had no naval experience whatsoever. Welles was pretty much in that boat. Lincoln joked that "Uncle Gideon" didn't know "bow from stern." Nonetheless, he was a good administrator. After a shaky start as Lincoln's secretary of the navy (while he was getting his sea legs, perhaps), Welles proved a capable man.

When Lincoln appointed him to the cabinet, Welles was fifty-eight. He was short and barrel chested, with a curly wig and a snow-white beard. Humorist Robert Newell (who used the comic alias "Orpheus C. Kerr"—that is, "Office Seeker") claimed that "the most interesting natural curiosity" in Washington was Gideon Welles's beard. Welles had enjoyed a long career in public service, having been an avid Andrew Jackson supporter and a loyal Democrat until his antislavery views drew him into the newly formed Republican Party. Lincoln's vice president, the forgotten Hannibal Hamlin, was a Maine man. After the election of 1860, Lincoln told Hamlin to pick a New Englander for the navy slot. He chose Welles, who was a newspaper editor in Hartford at the time. (The peculiar reasons why certain people are appointed to high posts does not inspire much confidence in human political systems.)

When the war began, the Confederacy had a more experienced navy secretary, Stephen Mallory. What he lacked in ships and sailors, Mallory made up for in keeping abreast of new developments in naval warfare. Thanks to him, the Confederacy was ahead of the Union in such innovations as ironclad ships, torpedoes, and even submarines. (The first sinking of a ship by a submarine was that of the Union's *Housatonic* by the Confederacy's *Hunley* near Charleston in February 1864.) The Union had some catching up to do. It also had to put its blockade into effect.

The blockade of Southern ports was Lincoln's idea, and not one that Welles supported. Yet some critics sneeringly called it the "Connecticut Plan," after Welles's home state. They said, justly, that it was a "paper blockade" Southerners could easily find their way around. But as the months passed, the blockade became increasingly effective, and more and more Southern ships and cargoes were captured. Welles then had the bright idea of capturing Port Royal, South Carolina, which gave the Union navy a base for capturing other Confederate ports. The landlubber was learning naval ways quickly.

Welles's right-hand man in the Navy Department (a man who *did* have a naval background) was Gustavus V. Fox. It was Fox who convinced Welles to use ironclad ships, which brings us to the Civil War's most famous naval battle.

On March 9, 1862, Welles went running

GIDEON
WELLES

1802–1878

to Lincoln with some news that led to a hasty cabinet meeting: the Confederacy had an iron-clad ship, the *Merrimack*. (The Rebels renamed that captured Union ship the CSS *Virginia*, so technically there was never a *Monitor-Merrimack* battle, but rather a *Monitor-Virginia* battle. But it was the name *Merrimack* that became lodged in everyone's consciousness.) Edwin Stanton, the always-fretful secretary of war, went into one of his frequent panics and ordered that sixty canal boats weighted with rocks be sunk in the Potomac to prevent the fearsome *Merrimack* from reaching Washington. Welles said (rightly) that Stanton had no business ordering the Navy Department around, and that Stanton's idea was stupid anyway. Lincoln agreed. In his paranoid tizzy, Stanton ranted that the Rebel ironclad "would destroy every vessel in the service" and then "disperse Congress, then destroy the Capitol and public buildings."

That was one of many amusing incidents that might have been forgotten had Welles not recorded it. The effort of Secretary of the Treasury Chase to get the entire cabinet to resign was also chronicled by Welles. So was Chase's attempt in 1864 to discredit the president and position himself as the logical candidate of the Republican Party. In fact, Welles's record of the egos, the pettiness, the malice, the envy, the tomfoolery, the blundering, and the shortsightedness of the cabinet make the success of Lincoln's presidency seem nothing short of a miracle. But then, Welles was prone to accentuating the negative. And also, no president has been fortunate enough to have a cabinet of flawless men. (Mostly, the members of Lincoln's cabinet were *honest* men, which counts for something in politics.)

Welles found that the army wasn't flawless either. He recorded (and here he was probably being as objective as he could) Lincoln's opinions about his generals, most of them failures until Grant and Sherman came along. Welles had his own opinions, usually right on target. "McClellan wishes to outgeneral the Rebels, but not to kill and destroy them," he wrote. "Halleck has suggested nothing, decided nothing, done nothing but scold and smoke and scratch his elbows."

Welles brought Lincoln the joyous news when Grant forced the surrender of Vicksburg. Lincoln was ecstatic. He was less than ecstatic (again, Welles was at hand to hear his reaction) when the Federals did not pursue and destroy Lee's army following Gettysburg.

After Lincoln's assassination, Andrew Johnson inherited the cabinet that included Welles. Welles proved to be one of Johnson's most loyal aides, although he thought Johnson might be slightly mad—a man who deliberately set himself up for impeachment hoping to play the political martyr.

In his diary, Welles confided that he (like Johnson) was hardly modern in his view of the races: "I am no advocate of social equality, nor do I labor for political or civil equality with the negro." Upon hearing of Southerners committing atrocities against freed slaves, he wrote that such accounts were "a mass of uncertain material . . . wholly unreliable . . . rumors, scandal, and gossip." On the issue of giving blacks the vote, he wrote, "Speakers are overrunning the country with their hateful harangues and excitable trash." Welles was typical of many Yankee statesmen; he was officially antislavery before and during the Civil War but hardly an equal-rights advocate afterward.

His three-volume diary remains priceless. It portrays Abraham Lincoln's cabinet warts and all (even the warts of Welles himself, though he worked to hide them, naturally). It could be called *The Curmudgeon's History of Civil War Washington*, and it is a darn good read.

Louis T. Wigfall, Confederate Politician and General
(1816–1874)

SENATOR SECESSIUS

WIGFALL DESERVES to be better known. After all, he helped bring the Confederacy into existence. He also helped ruin it. Generals get most of the attention, but politicians (particularly agitators like Wigfall) are the real bringers of war. The generals do their work because of (and often in spite of) the hot-blooded men who send them into battle.

Wigfall had a smidgen of military experience himself. He fought in the Seminole Wars in Florida for a few months. And he was a fighter by nature. Coming from the South Carolina plantation aristocracy as he did, *honor* was his favorite word and *duel* his second-favorite. The hot-tempered man fought in more than one; he killed one man, wounded another, and was wounded himself. Throughout his political life, he got a lot of mileage out of his reputation as a killer. No opponent could be sure that the black-haired, powerfully built man with those "eyes of the tiger" might not erupt once more.

Twenty-five years before secession came, Wigfall was pushing for it. South Carolina was, of course, the hotbed of such sentiment. But Wigfall had a rough time on his home turf. His reputation as a killer hung over his head, and he was constantly in debt, having quickly run through a sizable inheritance. (Wigfall was a notorious gambler, boozer, and brothel patron in his younger days.) He saw greener pastures in that new state, Texas. He started a law practice there and was elected a senator in 1859. This came in the wake of the hanging of abolitionist (or terrorist) John Brown, and Texas was in an anti-Northern frenzy. The openly secessionist Wigfall seemed the right choice.

He took his seat in the Thirty-sixth Congress, the last united session before the Civil War, though it didn't *feel* united in any way. Northern orators railed against Southern orators, and vice versa. It certainly wasn't dull, since this was an era that prized eloquent

speakers. (Put another way, it was a time when many blowhards became celebrities.) Wigfall, proud member of an oratorical society at South Carolina College, the Euphradians ("Dedicated to eloquence and correct speaking" was their motto), loved it. It allowed him to continue being a fighter, not a writer. "The pen is but a poor substitute for the tongue," he said. On one occasion, he delivered a four-hour off-the-cuff filibuster in the Senate.

In the fateful 1860 presidential race, Wigfall (like most secessionists) was gleeful that the Democratic Party split into Southern and Northern factions, guaranteeing the election of the Republican Lincoln. In the interim between Lincoln's election and inauguration, Wigfall gloried in his role as one who pushed his state to secede. On the Senate floor, he proclaimed that "a man who is distasteful to us has been elected, and we choose to consider that as a sufficient ground for leaving the Union, and we intend to leave the Union." He knew war was on the horizon after secession, but he didn't care. "Texas went out today," he said. "We have dissolved the Union; mend it if you can; cement it with blood." Perversely, after Texas seceded, Wigfall stayed on in the Senate, even though Texas was already sending representatives to the *Confederate* Congress. Clearly, he enjoyed those last days in Washington, taunting the Yankees. He

LOUIS T.
WIGFALL

1816–1874

justified remaining there by saying that Texas had not *officially* notified him that he was recalled. While still a United States senator, he established a Confederate army recruiting station in Baltimore.

But the egotistical orator knew his Washington days were numbered. And he wanted to be part of the new nation, preferably in the most colorful way possible. His opportunity came at Fort Sumter. On April 10, 1861, he became a military aide to Beauregard in Charleston. Before Beauregard sent anyone out to the besieged Federals at Sumter, Wigfall took it upon himself to negotiate unofficially. He dressed for drama—a red silk sash around his waist, brass spurs, a silk handkerchief around his neck. He chose his moment, when the Carolina guns had just shot down the Union flag over the fort. He went out in a rowboat, strode into the fort with a white handkerchief on the point of his sword, and met with the fort's commander, Robert Anderson. He admitted he had no authority for the meeting but said he was sure Beauregard would extend the same terms he was offering. Anderson assented. On the return crossing, Wigfall saw Beauregard's aides bearing the *official* terms of surrender. He was right—the terms were the same. Wigfall made the most of his moment in the spotlight. He was a hero in the Confederate capital, Montgomery, where a newspaper called him a "laborer in the vineyard of Southern rights."

The laborer in the vineyard cozied up to the Confederate president, Jefferson Davis. Davis made him (not quickly enough, in Wigfall's opinion) a brigadier general. Wigfall couldn't decide between politics and the army, so he chose both. He served in the Confederate Congress and at the same time commanded the First Texas Battalion.

But at heart, Wigfall was neither a soldier nor a politician but rather a critic and an agitator, both in the Union in former days and now in the Confederacy. Davis began to hear rumors that Wigfall, often under the influence of booze, was making speeches against him in Richmond hotels. (Wigfall never whispered if he could shout.) Wigfall also took the side of General Joe Johnston in his beef against Davis. In fact, he became an eager ear for any general who had a complaint against the president (and many did). He made no secret of his opinion that *he* knew how to handle the nation's military operations, while the stupid Davis obviously didn't. To make matters worse, Wigfall's wife became an open enemy of Mrs. Davis, whom she called a "coarse western woman" and "Queen Varina," which wasn't meant as a compliment.

Louis Wigfall holds a special place on the list of famous firsts. He was responsible for the first draft law in America, passed by the Confederate Congress in April 1862. Worse, he supported the infamous exemption for planters, who could hire substitutes. That exemption fed the popular notion that the Civil War was "a rich man's war and a poor man's fight."

The diarist Mary Chesnut wrote, "Wigfall, from whom we hoped so much, has only been destructive." She was right. One thing the Confederacy desperately needed was unity of purpose among its politicians. Thanks to Wigfall (and Davis, too, since both were extremely muleheaded), there was no harmony. For all his ego and bluster, Wigfall *did* have a better grasp of military strategy than Davis did. But *cooperation* was not a guiding principle in the Confederate capital.

When the war ended, Wigfall had reason to tremble. His reputation as a secessionist came back to haunt him. As a key mover behind secession, he was sure the Federals would punish him severely. In 1866, he fled to England. Since he had a reputation as a troublemaker, the British subsequently investigated him on suspicion of being an agitator in the Irish independence movement.

Wigfall returned to the United States in 1872, the anti-Confederate storm having blown over. He contributed to his friend Joe Johnston's self-praising memoirs. In retort, Jefferson Davis's self-praising memoirs laid blame on his administration's political opponents—chief among them Wigfall—for helping lose the war.

William L. Yancey, Secessionist and Confederate Diplomat

(1814–1863)

HE WHO SPLIT THINGS

"THE MAN and the hour have met." That is one of the most frequently quoted lines of the Civil War, and it was uttered by Alabama secessionist William Lowndes Yancey when he introduced the Confederacy's first (and, as it turned out, *only*) president, Jefferson Davis, to a cheering crowd in Montgomery, Alabama. Yancey's words have earned him at least a mention in the history books, but he was in fact a fixture on the Southern (and secessionist) scene for decades. He was one of the most notorious of the "fire-eaters," those obsessive, anti-North, proslavery, pro-South, anti-

Federal politicians, editors, and speakers who formed the opposition to the just-as-fanatical abolitionists of the North. Fanatics and obsessives help bring about revolutions (consider Patrick Henry and Samuel Adams in the 1770s), but once the process is under way and a new nation is formed, they prove pretty useless. That was certainly true in Yancey's case.

He was an orator in an age that prized eloquent speaking. Everyone, even his enemies, agreed that he had a beautiful, even *sweet*, voice. He was one of those lucky men who could speak very loudly without seeming to bellow. And the one theme he loved to speak on was the South—that is, a South left alone by meddlesome abolitionists, a South that had slaves and (if things went as Yancey hoped) always would. He himself owned many, largely thanks to his wealthy wife. He had painful memories of his self-righteous stepfather, a preacher and—horrors!—an abolitionist.

Yancey had a temper that got him into trouble with a relative of his wife; he killed the man in a scuffle and served three months in jail. Among plantation aristocrats, this was a plus, not a minus. It meant he was a man who would defend his honor. He said the episode should serve as "a warning to others who feel like browbeating a Yancey." Later, while serving in Congress, he fought a duel with another congressman.

Yancey never liked Congress. He lacked the tact and the willingness to compromise that make good (or at least successful) politicians. He came to hate political parties in general. Like his idol, John C. Calhoun, he urged Southerners to avoid party labels and pursue an independent, pro-Southern course.

In the meantime, his reputation as a speaker grew. One observer described his speeches as "seasoned with the salt of argument, the vinegar of sarcasm, the pepper of wit, and the genuine champagne of eloquence." He learned to control his notorious temper and channel it into fine language. And he sometimes made sense. He claimed that the sole function of government was "the greatest good for the greatest number, consistent with the inalienable rights of the minority." (The minority he had in mind was, of course, Southerners.)

Like most men driven by obsession, Yancey found it hard to relax. Once, his family enjoyed a pleasant seaside vacation on Alabama's Gulf coast, but Yancey spoke of it as "dull, very dull to me." He didn't feel truly alive unless he was agitating.

Not surprisingly, the renowned secessionist was featured at the Democratic Convention in Charleston in April 1860. He and some

WILLIAM L.
YANCEY

1814–1863

fellow "fire-eaters" pushed for a "Southern platform," insisting that any Democratic candidate for president *must* be openly proslavery. The platform was rejected, and Yancey stormed out of the gathering, followed by several other delegates. He had put himself in a win-win situation: either his platform passed (it didn't) or he would split the Democratic Party (bingo!). He then spent the months before the November election on a national speaking tour. He drew a crowd of twenty thousand in New Orleans and held up the Crescent City as an example of a Southern metropolis that could survive very well without the United States, thank you.

Needless to say, things happened exactly as Yancey might have predicted. The Democrats split (running both a Northern and a Southern candidate), the Republican Lincoln won, and states (including Yancey's Alabama) began to secede.

It was not long afterward that he spoke his famous words regarding Jefferson Davis: "The man and the hour have met. We may now hope that prosperity, honor, and victory await his administration." They didn't. That was precisely the secessionists' biggest flaw: they never imagined that a separate Southern nation might actually collapse.

Davis felt that Yancey was owed a political favor. Stupidly, he appointed him as a diplomat to England and France, with the mission of getting those nations to recognize the Confederacy's independence. (A man with a notorious temper should *not* be made a diplomat, as anyone knows.) After less than a year, he returned with sad news: "We cannot look for any sympathy or help from abroad. We must rely on ourselves alone." Both Yancey and Davis had believed that Europeans' need for Southern cotton would gain their support. No dice. Cotton diplomacy was a failure.

Yancey did become a Confederate senator. One day on the Senate floor, he and Benjamin Hill of Georgia exchanged insults (eloquent ones, no doubt). Hill threw an inkstand at Yancey, cutting his face. Before they could fight, other senators separated them. The incident is a symbol of how the Confederate Congress functioned.

Like fellow "fire-eater" Louis Wigfall, Yancey became a vocal anti-Davis man. He blamed Davis for everything that went wrong in the Confederacy, including mosquitoes and humidity. Fortunately for Davis, Yancey died in 1863. (It was probably fortunate for Yancey as well, since he didn't live to see the Confederacy defeated.) Oddly, just before he died, he tried to heal the breach with Davis. Yancey had worked to restore Mount Vernon, George

Washington's home. In gratitude, the home's overseers gave him a gift—Washington's spyglass. Yancey willed it to Davis.

The Yancey name lingers in an odd place: Brazil. Two of his sons joined other former Confederates there to build a colony named Confederado. Yanceys still live there.

Select Bibliography

Bridges, Hal. *Lee's Maverick General: Daniel Harvey Hill*. New York: McGraw-Hill, 1961.

Catton, Bruce. *Mr. Lincoln's Army*. New York: Doubleday, 1952.

Chesnut, Mary Boykin. *A Diary from Dixie*. Cambridge, Mass.: Harvard University Press, 1980.

Coulter, E. Merton. *The Confederate States of America, 1861–1865*. Baton Rouge: Louisiana State University Press, 1950.

Davis, Burke. *Gray Fox: Robert E. Lee and the Civil War*. New York: Rinehart, 1956.

Davis, Jefferson. *The Rise and Fall of the Confederate Government*. 2 vols. New York: Appleton, 1881.

Douglas, Henry Kyd. *I Rode with Stonewall*. Chapel Hill: University of North Carolina Press, 1940.

Dowdey, Clifford. *Death of a Nation: The Story of Lee and His Men at Gettysburg*. New York: Knopf, 1958.

———. *The Land They Fought For: The Story of the South as the Confederacy*. Garden City, N.Y.: Doubleday, 1955.

Eaton, Clement. *A History of the Southern Confederacy*. New York: Macmillan, 1954.

———. *Jefferson Davis*. New York: Free Press, 1977.

Foote, Shelby. *Stars in Their Courses: The Gettysburg Campaign*. New York: Modern Library, 1994.

Freeman, Douglas Southall. *Lee's Lieutenants*. 3 vols. New York: Scribner's, 1944.

———. *R. E. Lee*. 4 vols. New York: Scribner's, 1935.

Harwell, Richard B., ed. *The Confederate Reader: How the South Saw the War*. 1957. Reprint, New York: Dover Publications, 1989.

Hattaway, Herman, and Archer Jones. *How the North Won: A Military History of the Civil War*. Urbana: University of Illinois Press, 1983.

Hood, John B. *Advance and Retreat: Personal Experiences in the United States and Confederate States Armies*. 1880. Reprint, Bloomington: Indiana University Press, 1959.

Horn, Stanley. *The Army of Tennessee*. Norman: University of Oklahoma Press, 1941.

Johnson, Paul. *A History of the American People*. New York: HarperCollins, 1997.

Kane, Harnett T. *Spies for the Blue and Gray*. New York: Hanover House, 1954.

Kerby, Robert L. *Kirby Smith's Confederacy: The Transmississippi South*. New York: Columbia University Press, 1972.

King, Alvy L. *Louis T. Wigfall: Southern Fire-eater*. Baton Rouge: Louisiana State University Press, 1970.

Leckie, Robert. *None Died in Vain: The Saga of the American Civil War*. New York: HarperCollins, 1990.

Lytle, Andrew. *Bedford Forrest and His Critter Company*. New York: Minton, Balch, 1931.

McPherson, James M. *Battle Cry of Freedom: The Era of the Civil War*. New York: Oxford University Press, 1988.

McWhiney, Grady. *Braxton Bragg and Confederate Defeat*. New York: Columbia University Press, 1969.

Mosby, John S. *Memoirs*. 1917. Reprint, Nashville, Tenn.: J. S. Sanders, 1995.

O'Connor, Richard. *Hood: Cavalier General*. New York: Prentice-Hall, 1949.

———. *Thomas: Rock of Chickamauga*. New York: Prentice-Hall, 1948.

Osborne, Charles C. *Jubal: The Life and Times of Jubal A. Early*. Chapel Hill, N.C.: Algonquin, 1992.

Parks, Joseph H. *General E. Kirby Smith, C.S.A.* Baton Rouge: Louisiana State University Press, 1954.

Patrick, Rembert W. *Jefferson Davis and His Cabinet*. Baton Rouge: Louisiana State University Press, 1944.

Robertson, James I., Jr. *A. P. Hill: The Story of a Confederate Warrior*. New York: Random House, 1987.

———. *Civil War Virginia: Battleground for a Nation*. Charlottesville: University Press of Virginia, 1991.

———. *Stonewall Jackson: The Man, the Soldier, the Legend*. New York: Macmillan, 1997.

Sandburg, Carl. *Abraham Lincoln: The Prairie Years and the War Years*. 1-vol. edition. New York: Galahad Books, 1954.

Schultz, Duane. *Quantrill's War: The Life and Times of William Clarke Quantrill*. New York: St. Martin's, 1996.

Siepel, Kevin H. *Rebel: The Life and Times of John Singleton Mosby*. New York: St. Martin's, 1983.

Symonds, Craig L. *Joseph E. Johnston*. New York: Norton, 1992.

Taylor, Richard. *Destruction and Reconstruction*. Edited by Richard Harwell. New York: Longmans, Green, 1955.

Thomas, Emory M. *Bold Dragoon: The Life of J. E. B. Stuart*. New York: Harper & Row, 1986.

———. *The Confederate Nation, 1861–1865*. New York: Harper & Row, 1979.

Vandiver, Frank E. *Mighty Stonewall*. 1957. Reprint, College Station: Texas A & M University Press, 1988.

————. *Their Tattered Flags: The Epic of the Confederacy*. 1970. Reprint, College Station: Texas A & M University Press, 1987.

Walther, Eric H. *The Fire-Eaters*. Baton Rouge: Louisiana State University Press, 1992.

Warner, Ezra. *Generals in Gray*. Baton Rouge: Louisiana State University Press, 1959.

Wert, Jeffrey D. *Custer*. New York: Simon & Schuster, 1996.

Wiley, Bell Irvin. *The Life of Johnny Reb*. 1943. Reprint, Baton Rouge: Louisiana State University Press, 1978.

Index